TWO FAT LADIES
FULL THROTTLE

TWO FAT LADIES
FULL THROTTLE

Jennifer Paterson and
Clarissa Dickson Wright

Clarkson Potter/Publishers
New York

NOTE: ALL RECIPES SERVE 4
UNLESS OTHERWISE STATED

Published by Clarkson N. Potter, Inc.,
201 East 50th Street, New York,
New York 10022.
Member of the Crown Publishing Group.

Random House, Inc. New York, Toronto,
London, Sydney, Auckland

www.randomhouse.com

CLARKSON POTTER, POTTER and
colophon are trademarks of
Clarkson N. Potter, Inc.

Printed in Singapore

Library of Congress Cataloging-in-
Publication Data is available upon request.

ISBN 0 09 186710 X

10 9 8 7 6 5 4 3 2 1

First American Edition

Designed by Alison Shackleton
Food photography by James Murphy
Food styling by Alison Birch
Styling by Róisín Nield

Acknowledgments

To Pat Llewellyn, our own beloved Dr. Frankenstein, who we really, really love and adore! (She made us say the last bit.)

Peter Gillbe, tireless in his efforts. We've never seen jet-lag worn so lightly, and Diogenes could die happy.

Lesley—the blessed return of Lesley has saved all our sanities.

Darling Spike, our cameraman/director, who has brought a whole new toy box to our nursery.

Bridget, our coordinator, without whom nothing would ever move and who could do the equestrian stunts to boot.

Polly, beloved researcher, known as "Polly who is not going to put the kettle on any more." Our beautiful lioness is leaving us for higher things.

Guy (de Montfort), our new little bambi (6'3"), a welcome, angelic addition and not just a pretty face but a great researcher, too.

Corinne, a paragon of efficiency and, as Jennifer said, when she says "Talk to you later" you know, unfortunately, that she means it!

(Saint) Luke, our other cameraman, still the finest croquet player on the team.

Sara, our valiant camera operator, who risked life and limb with bees and oarsmen alike.

Louis, naughty little Louis, "lucky 21-year-old toy boy," the billiardo king.

Billy, our beloved team heart-throb.

Rex, dearly beloved, who would be totally perfect if he would only eat meat.

Our editor, Paul Ratcliffe, a tireless perfectionist who makes sure our mistakes remain on the cutting room floor.

Ginny, a madonna, even in her apron, and with the temperament to boot.

Elaine—how can one work so hard on a diet of mini-cheddars and doughnuts?

Dear Basil Comely, genius as ever, and proud father of the book title, Full Throttle.

Mark Thompson, "darling Ignatius," thank God for a Papist controller.

Thanks to Adam Kemp and Jane Root, our stalwart supporters at the BBC.

And thanks to Fiona MacIntyre, Penny Simpson, and Isabel Duffy, the still long-suffering gang at Ebury Press.

CONTENTS

INTRODUCTION

*Outside Paddy Coyne's pub in Ireland, with the publican and
lobster fishermen.*

It wasn't until halfway through my conversation with Clarissa that I realized my exciting news was going down like a soufflé in a draft.

"America?" she barked down the phone. "You don't really expect me to go to America?" I should have known. After vegetarians and supermarkets, Clarissa holds the home of the hamburger responsible for everything that's wrong with the modern world—including fast food, political correctness, and plastic surgery. But for British television producers, the merest whiff of American interest causes ripples of excitement and inspires the construction of lavish castles in the air. So if you're offered a promotional tour by a broadcaster, you only hes-itate long enough to throw some clothes into a bag and run to the airport. Clarissa, however, was determined to stick to her principles.

I was confident of Jennifer though. I knew she'd want to go. She'd lived in the States once and had rather enjoyed it. She's also a big fan of old American films.

"I would like to see Hollywood," she said, "but isn't Los Angeles rather hot? You know I can't stand the heat and think of my poor feet." (Jennifer had spent the last month with each toe wrapped in banana skin to cure her warts.) Desperate measures were called for. "But Clarissa's dying to go," I explained, silently offering up a prayer for absolution.

"Jennifer's dying to go," I explained to Clarissa. "She says she has to see Hollywood before she dies." I made a mental note that my earlier prayer should hold good for two lies rather than just the one.

"Americans are intrigued by good manners, in part because they don't have any." We were on the airplane going to America. Clarissa was on my right, reading aloud from *The Xenophobe's Guide To The Americans.* On my left sat Jennifer, whose dreams of Hollywood had taken a battering. She'd just seen *Jurassic Park* and was very confused. "Who was that fat man in the laboratory? Do you know?" she asked me. She sought assistance from the air hostess. "Have you seen *Jurassic Park*? Did you understand what that fat man was stealing?" That neither of us could tell her confirmed Hollywood was a very different place from the days of Norma Desmond when it was only the sun that went down on Sunset Boulevard. "Why don't they make films like they used to?" Jennifer wanted to know. We were at 30,000 feet but I could still feel my heart sinking. Even a fistful of dollars wasn't going to make this trip worthwhile.

When we arrived in New York there were several huge limousines lined up outside the terminal. "Ugh. Americans have to do everything bigger than everyone else." Clarissa grumped. "So ostentatious and vulgar," Jennifer agreed. At this, the driver of the biggest limousine, less a car and more of a living room on wheels, got out

with a board with the Ladies' names on. "I suppose we'll just have to put up with it," said Clarissa, disappearing inside. Seconds later Jennifer's voice boomed out of the darkness. "My dear, there's a bar in here." I breathed an American-sized sigh of relief—things were looking up.

The whole of the U.S. seemed to have developed Fatladymania—everywhere they went people were genuinely delighted to see them. Live chat shows, book signings, interviews for newspapers and magazines were all crammed into our rather breathless timetable. At our book signing in New York City, people were lining up around the block. Some had brought presents. One woman had learned the program credits off by heart—she reeled off the names of everyone on the production team and wanted to know all about them. "What does Luke Cardiff look like? And Polly Livingston? Is she married?"

We were whisked to Los Angeles to stay at the palatial Chateau Marmont. My suite was so enormous I got lost on the way to the bedroom. We were sitting in the bar before dinner one evening when I became rather excited—Keanu Reeves was sitting at the other side of the room. "Oh for goodness sake Patricia you're so star struck," Jennifer said. "Who on earth is Keanu Reeves?" Clarissa wanted to know, so I pointed him out as discreetly as I could. "Oh him," she said, waving enthusiastically. "He's the nice young man I've been chatting with beside the

Jennifer and Clarissa trip the light fantastic at Kylemore Abbey in Co. Galway.

pool all afternoon. He never mentioned he was an actor. In fact, we talked about vegetables."

On our last evening in New York, we went to a wonderful Japanese restaurant called Nobu. We were treated like queens by the maitre d' who was clearly besotted. He kept ordering delicious morsels for us from the kitchen and introducing us proudly to his regular diners. One gentleman we met worked for Steven Spielberg, the director of *Jurassic Park*. Jennifer leapt in without pausing for breath. "Oh good. Who was that fat man in the laboratory? Do you know?

What was he stealing?" He seemed a little taken aback, but after ten minutes all was clear.

For a program that most people thought would not get many viewers outside the London viewing areas, it's been a bumper year. The series has sold all over the world (it's great with Hebrew subtitles but even better dubbed into Japanese) and the Ladies seem to be more in demand than ever. They even got invited to one of the Prime Minister and Mrs. Blair's famous media parties at Downing Street. Clarissa didn' t want to go as she's still fuming about the beef on the bone ban, so I got to be Cinderella. We had a delightful evening, marred only by the fact Jennifer wasn't allowed to smoke. For some reason, every news program needs footage to cover a story about Labour Party sleaze uses footage of Jennifer meeting Mrs. Blair. I fail to see what's so sleazy about an elderly Catholic lady who's a spinster of the parish of Westminster swapping recipes with one of the country's leading senior lawyers (although if the government brings in a tax cut on motorbikes with sidecars, they'd have every right to be suspicious).

This book accompanies our third television series. We've had another summer traveling around the country to weird and wonderful locations, praying for sunny weather. Who knows where we'll be next, but we hope that you will be watching.

Pat Llewellyn
Series Producer

SOUPS AND APPETIZERS

This is the life! Jennifer and Clarissa go punting in Cambridge.

CLARISSA WRITES: Our TV program is about menus this year, and I would like you to keep the thought of the menu with you at all times while reading this book.

The first course is many people's favorite part of the meal, indeed there was once a highly successful London restaurant that served nothing but appetizers and desserts. In many ways, the first course is like a TV trailer or an advertizement: You want to grab the attention of your guests away from their drinks and their predinner chat and refocus them onto the fact they are now sitting down to enjoy your food. If you don't do this you will feel like the chef in the Saki story who ran amok and drowned the bandleader in the soup tureen because everyone was listening to the music and ignoring his efforts!

Carry the concept of your whole menu with you at all times. If your main course is light, then you can afford a more robust appetizer. When we were cooking for the Cambridge University Rowing Eight, the main course was a fairly light rabbit dish of mine with a sort of hot salad in the form of Jennifer's Peas with Lettuce. So, knowing how hungry they would be, we gave them a substantial bean soup full of Spanish sausages, ham hocks, and other good things (for less hearty appetites this would make a very good main course) as the appetizer. The capacity of your guests is another thing to be considered—those

Clarissa goes digital during a tea break.

glorious golden young men will grow into dilettantes whose ravished palates and sensitive digestions need both titillating and nurturing. Incindentally, the oarsmen were so fit that when we were trying to keep pace with them on the towpath the bike could barely keep up! It gives a whole different picture to the historic use of water transport to imagine Henry VIII's great gilded barge powered by the likes of those young giants. So much nicer than our dear present Queen's gas-powered taxi!

Some of the best appetizers are, of course, the simplest. As I write we are just entering the asparagus season, and nothing can be nicer than well-cooked, new season asparagus with melted butter or hollandaise sauce. However, as Jennifer pointed out in last year's Christmas special, we don't get paid to tell you to serve a plate of smoked salmon. In cold weather, soups are good value, but be careful with cold summer soups—in Scotland, for example, many people don't seem to like them much and many men think they are a mere frivolity.

I like my appetizers to have a punch, and because nowadays many ingredients are so flavorless that you have to work around them rather than with them, the salmon mousse I served to the lawyers of Lincoln's Inn had blue cheese in it. They loved it but I would not spoil good wild salmon by using that recipe.

Above all don't lose sight of your menu, focus on the perspective of the meal when choosing your appetizer and remember the colors of the meal—nothing is worse than an all white menu, and the different courses should appeal to the eye as well as the stomach.

Jennifer enjoys filming in another great British summer.

Cosmopolitan

This is not strictly an appetizer, it is a cocktail, but certainly something to start a meal with a bang. I was given the recipe by Alan Kearney, the well-known New York barman, on a recent trip to New York City. He made one for Patricia, our beloved producer, upon whom they seemed to have a very strange effect. She took to dancing with strangers in the hotel bar and refused to go to bed, very unlike her. Delicious—but proceed with caution.

EACH DRINK SHOULD BE MADE OF:
½ fresh lime
2 parts citron vodka
1 part Cointreau
¾ part cranberry juice

Squeeze the ½ lime into an ice cold martini glass. Combine the vodka, Cointreau, and cranberry juice in a metal cocktail shaker. Shake very well and strain into the martini glass.

JP

Baden Leek Soup

This recipe comes from Baden Baden, the well-known German health spa, and it is a nourishing comforting soup. The "honest toun" of Musselburgh, in Scotland, where I live is famous for its leeks, even the ancient Romans praised and exported Musselburgh leeks. It was only in this century that the species was registered and named by the great botanist and horticulturist, Mr. Scarlett. It is a soup I often make with our excellent leeks.

4 leeks
4 tablespoons (½ stick) butter
2 onions, finely chopped
1 quart good chicken stock
salt and freshly ground pepper
7 cups milk
1 potato, cooked and mashed
¼ pound cooked ham, chopped
½ cup light cream
finely chopped parsley, to serve

Trim and wash the leeks, leaving some of the green. Slice thinly. Melt the butter in a large pan and sauté the leeks and onions until soft. Add stock and seasoning, bring to a boil and simmer for 15 minutes.

Mix the milk and mashed potato together and stir into the broth. Return to a boil and leave to thicken. Remove from the heat and stir in the ham and cream. Return to the heat but do not allow to boil. Serve sprinkled with parsley.

CDW

Beet Soup

This is not a real Russian beet soup, but it has a wonderful color nevertheless. It is quite filling and suitable as a supper dish with very little to follow, or you might serve it chilled after removing any fat that rises to the top.

3¾ cups chicken stock
½ pound beets, peeled and chopped
1½ cups potatoes, peeled and chopped
scant 1 cup carrots, peeled and chopped
scant 1 cup parsnips, peeled and chopped
½ cup chopped celery
1 leek, green top and white parts finely sliced and reserved separately
1 large onion, chopped
1 garlic clove, finely chopped
¼ cup goose or chicken fat or 1 tablespoon vegetable oil
1 teaspoon herbes de Provence or Italian seasoning
2 tablespoons (¼ stick) butter
1 tablespoon finely chopped parsley

OPTIONAL:
tomato paste
orange juice
red wine
sherry
sour cream

Bring the stock to a boil. Add the beets, potatoes, carrots, parsnips, celery, and green leek tops and simmer for about 1 hour. (Beets take a long time to cook!)

In the meanwhile, fry the onions, white part of leek, and garlic in the fat or oil in a skillet until the onions begin to brown, stirring continuously. Add the herbs and fry a little longer. Add these ingredients to the saucepan and just bring to a boil.

Allow to cool for 5 minutes, add the chopped parsley and then purée in a food processor or blender.

You may enhance the color of the soup by adding tomato paste—and give flavor by adding either orange juice, red wine, or sherry. A swirl of sour cream may be added when serving.

JP

Asturian Bean and Sausage Soup

My mad, wild friends, the Herbie boys, from the delicatessen of that name in Edinburgh, gave me a mercillo, or Spanish blood sausage, and in return I gave them this recipe. Do not confuse Asturia, which is a Spanish Kingdom, with the land of lederhosen. This is a good rib-sticking soup and a meal in itself.

1½ cups dried white beans, soaked in water overnight
7-ounce ham hock, soaked in water for 1 hour
5 ounces pork belly, on the bone
5 ounces pork belly, cubed
3 fresh mercillos or other blood sausages
2 or 3 chorizo sausages
1½ pounds dark green cabbage
1 pound potatoes
salt and freshly ground black pepper
pinch of paprika, optional

Put all the ingredients, except the cabbage and potatoes, into a pan and cover with water. Skim as the water comes to a boil and cook for 1 hour, or until the beans are almost tender.

Cut up the cabbage quite finely and bring to a boil in a saucepan of salted water. Drain. Remove the meat bones, returning any shreds of meat to the pan with the sliced sausages. Season with plenty of black pepper and salt to taste. Add the cabbage and potatoes, and more liquid if necessary to cover them comfortably. Simmer until the potatoes are tender and check the seasoning.

If your chorizos are not very spicy, add some paprika. Serve in big bowls with country bread.

CDW

Fish Soup

This is a simple soup, very suitable for the days in Lent. It has a good flavor and a sufficient feel of penitence about it to please the most rigid of worshipers.

Serves 3-4

1 large onion
1 garlic clove, chopped
1 celery stalk, chopped
1 carrot, peeled and chopped
1 tomato, skinned and chopped
1 tablespoon olive oil
2 tablespoons (¼ stick) butter
pinch each of thyme, sage, dill, and saffron
1 large cod's head
1 bay leaf
4 cups water
1 tablespoon tomato paste
1 tablespoon raw rice
salt and freshly ground pepper
croutons, to serve

Fry the onion, garlic, chopped celery, chopped carrot, and tomato in the olive oil and butter until the onions are opaque. Add the herbs and saffron and fry for a little longer. Add the cod's head, bay leaf, and water. Bring to a boil, lower the heat, and simmer for about 1 hour.

Strain the soup into another saucepan, add the tomato paste and rice, and boil for 10 minutes. Add salt and pepper to taste. Fry some croutons in olive oil and serve with the soup.

JP

Chicken and Ginger Soup

It is difficult to find a proper boiling fowl these days. The best places to look are Chinese grocers, where they are called endearingly "old hen," or Halal butchers. It seems to me the ethnic communities in Britain have priorities the rest of us would be well encouraged to emulate. In my recent visit to Smithfield Market, in London's East End, for filming, I was interested to notice the large number of Chinese and West Indians who were painstakingly choosing such vital ingredients as pigs' trotters and heads or old hens. This is an Asian-style soup and tastes nicely of ginger.

1 boiling fowl (old hen)
2 quarts water
1 tablespoon oil
1 onion, finely sliced
1 tablespoon finely shredded gingerroot
1½ pounds Chinese leaves or spinach, shredded
soy sauce
2 eggs, beaten

Cut the chicken into pieces and boil for 1 hour in salted water. Strain and reserve the stock. Remove the skin and bones from the chicken and shred the flesh. If the stock does not have enough flavor, return the bones to it and boil to reduce, then strain again.

Heat the oil in a large saucepan and cook the onion gently until soft. Add the gingerroot and fry for 1 minute. Strain the chicken stock into this mixture, and add the shredded chicken and Chinese leaves or spinach. Simmer gently for 10 minutes. Beat the eggs and pour them into the soup, stirring as you pour. Serve at once.

CDW

Green Rice Soup

This delicious and unusual soup comes from Sri Owen's brilliant *Rice Book*. The sorrel gives it a tart refreshing taste, and as it is an antiscorbutic is a better way of imbibing vitamin C than chewing tablets. If you have no sorrel, use spinach or chard. Make sure you use a good, rich stock and freshly grated nutmeg.

2 tablespoons olive oil or
2 tablespoons (¼ stick) butter
3 shallots or 1 onion, chopped
1 garlic clove, chopped
¼ teaspoon grated nutmeg
pinch of salt
¼ teaspoon ground white pepper
5 cups stock
½ cup cooked white rice
6 ounces sorrel, spinach or chard, well washed

In a large saucepan, heat the oil or butter and sweat the shallots or onion and garlic. Add the nutmeg, salt, and pepper and pour in the stock. I use chicken stock but a good-flavored vegetable, pork, or veal stock will do as well.

Bring to a boil and add the rice. Simmer for 10 minutes. Add the sorrel or other greens and simmer for a further 4 minutes. Transfer to a blender and blend until smooth; if too thick add a little more stock. Cook for a few minutes longer, stirring frequently. Serve hot or cold.

CDW

Garbure

This is a French cabbage soup, not unlike the Italian minestrone but without the pasta. A good hearty meal in itself. The goose fat gives an inimitable flavor and can be bought in cans in good grocery stores or delicatessens.

1-pound piece of boneless, uncooked ham
5 cups water
1 large potato
1 small rutabaga
1 carrot
1 bouquet garni
1 bay leaf
1 large onion, finely chopped
2 garlic cloves, finely chopped
¼ cup goose fat or
1 tablespoon each of vegetable oil and butter
pinch of fresh thyme
3¼ cups shredded cabbage
1 tablespoon chopped parsley
salt and freshly ground pepper
croutons, to serve

Put the ham in a large saucepan. Add the water and bring to a boil. Lower the heat and simmer for 30-40 minutes, or until the ham is cooked. Remove the ham from the pan and set aside, retaining the water for cooking the vegetables.

In the meanwhile, peel the potato, rutabaga, and carrot and chop each into smallish chunks. Cook these root vegetables in the reserved ham water with the bouquet garni and the bay leaf. Gently fry the onion and garlic in the goose fat and add a pinch of thyme.

When the root vegetables are cooked until tender, remove the bouquet garni from the pan but add the fried onions, garlic, and thyme and stir. Purée in a food processor or blender. Put this soup back in the saucepan, bring to a boil and add the shredded cabbage. Cook for a further 10 minutes. Add the chopped parsley. Fry the croutons in some more of the goose fat or oil and butter. Cut the pieces of ham into small chunks, place in serving bowls, and ladle the soup over. Serve with croutons.

JP

Potage Billy By

This recipe was invented for the sole purpose of pandering to American snobbishness about eating mussels with their fingers. A very good customer by the name of William Brand of Ciro's in Deauville, France, having invited some American friends to lunch asked the chef, Pierre Franey, to concoct a soup which included the juices of the mussels but not the mussels themselves. It was such a success it became established as Potage Billy Brand. Discretion, eventually, changed the name to Potage Billy By or sometimes Billy Bi.

2 pounds mussels
1 tablespoon steel-cut oats
4 shallots, chopped
2 celery stalks, chopped
4 tablespoons (½ stick) butter
¼ cup dry white wine
1 bouquet garni
1 bay leaf
6 black peppercorns
5 cups fish stock
2½ cups heavy cream
2 egg yolks
1 tablespoon chopped parsley
salt and freshly ground pepper

Wash and scrape the mussels, making sure the beard is removed. Leave for a couple of hours, or overnight, in salted water to which you have added the oats.

In a large saucepan, fry the shallots and celery in the butter for about 3 minutes before adding the dry white wine, bouquet garni, bay leaf, peppercorns, and mussels. Cook over high heat, covered, shaking the saucepan very often until the mussels open; this should take about 10 minutes.

Remove the mussels and their shells, returning any liquid to the pan. Strain the liquid through a strainer lined with cheesecloth into a saucepan. Add the fish stock, bring to the boil, and allow to simmer for about 30 minutes. Allow to cool.

Add the cream to the fish stock and reheat, bringing just to a boil, stirring continuously. Cool for 2 minutes. Ladle a little liquid into the egg yolks and whisk. Add this to the soup with the chopped parsley, stirring well. Add salt and pepper if need be and serve with the cooked mussels.

JP

Brazil Nut Soup

When I was six my father took my mother and me to Brazil. We stayed there for several months as he wanted to learn about snake venom. I remember when I came home the nuns asked me what I had liked best and I said *Fejoiada*. Brazil was, I think, the place where I first realized different countries have different food. This is a strange soup and to me very reminiscent of the country.

12 ounces shelled brazil nuts
2 quarts good chicken stock
4 tablespoons (½ stick) unsalted butter
⅓ cup all-purpose flour
salt and freshly ground pepper
¼ teaspoon ground mace
1 cup heavy cream
2 pomegranates

Toast the nuts for 10 minutes in a preheated 400°F oven, turning occasionally. Cool and rub the skins off the nuts. Grind finely in a food processor.

Heat the stock in a large pan. Add a ladle of stock to the nuts in the food processor a ladle at a time, pulsing until smooth. In a saucepan, melt the butter and stir in the flour. Add the remaining hot stock a little at a time and season with salt, pepper, and mace. Stir in the cream. Simmer gently for 20 minutes. If the soup is too thick, stir in more cream.

Extract the juice from 1 of the pomegrantes by slicing it in half, scooping out the seeds of the fruit into a strainer placed over a bowl and then crushing them with the back of a wooden spoon. Add the juice to the soup. Serve the soup in warm plates, and top with seeds from the remaining pomegranate.

CDW

Welsh Rarebit Soufflés

I think nearly everybody enjoys cheese dishes. This is a variation on the original Welsh rarebit, which was, in fact, pure toasted cheese cooked in the oven. This makes a very good supper dish, or when cut into small pieces, an excellent morsel to go with drinks.

2 cups grated really good sharp cheddar cheese
4 eggs, separated
1 teaspoon dry English mustard
Worcestershire sauce
hot-pepper sauce
salt and freshly ground pepper
4 large slices of good white bread

Place the cheese in a bowl, beat in 3 egg yolks (use the fourth one in something else), the mustard, a good shake of Worcestershire sauce and the hot-pepper sauce, and season to taste. Toast the bread.

Beat the 4 egg whites until they stand in stiff peaks. Add a spoonful or so to the cheese mixture, then gently fold the rest of them into the bowl. Put the toasts into a baking dish and pour the mixture over them. Bake in a preheated 450°F oven for 10 minutes until brown and risen. Serve at once with a salad or spinach on the side.

JP

Red Peppers Stuffed with Eggplant Purée

Eggplant, aubergine, and melanzane are all the same vegetable in different languages, and a favorite of mine. It can be used in so many ways, from delicious fritters to poor man's caviar. These bell peppers stuffed with purée give you a double whammy and really are the full monty.

3 medium-sized eggplants
3 tablespoons olive oil
1 large garlic clove, finely chopped
juice of 1 large lemon
3 tablespoons chopped parsley
salt and freshly ground black pepper
4 large bell peppers
toasted bread fingers, to serve

Make the eggplant purée by broiling the eggplants until the skins are charred and starting to blister, which should mean the pulp inside is soft. Leave to cool slightly, then remove the skin by rubbing gently under cold water. Purée the eggplant flesh with 2 tablespoons of the olive oil and then blend in the garlic, lemon juice, 2 tablespoons of the parsley, salt and pepper. Pour the purée into a bowl.

Cut the bell peppers in half lengthwise, remove the stems and seeds, and brush the inside with the remaining olive oil. Bake in a preheated 350°F oven for 30 minutes.

About 15 minutes before serving, fill the pepper halves with the eggplant purée, and replace in the oven to warm through. After 15 minutes remove the peppers from the oven, sprinkle with remaining parsley, and serve with plain toasted bread fingers.

JP

Mushroom Pasties

This is a medieval recipe from Maggie Black's excellent *The Medieval Cookbook*, which she wrote for the British Museum Press. I first served these patties at a lunch which I cooked for dear Michael Bateman and *The Independent on Sunday*, where they had great acclaim. These are excellent for drinks parties or a buffet.

FOR THE PASTRY DOUGH:
2 cups all-purpose flour
½ teaspoon salt
6 tablespoons (¾ stick) butter
6 tablespoons lard or vegetable shortening

FOR THE FILLING:
1 pound Paris or button mushrooms
2 tablespoon olive oil
½ cup grated cheddar cheese
salt and freshly ground black pepper
¼ teaspoon dry mustard
1 egg, beaten

To make the pastry dough, sift the flour and salt into a bowl and cut in the butter and lard. Press into a dough, adding a little ice water if necessary to bind.

Roll out two-thirds of the pastry dough and use to line eight small deep muffin pans. Chill for at least 30 minutes. Trim off the mushroom stems, put the tops into a strainer, and dip the mushrooms into boiling water. Drain them, then pat dry, and chop. Put them into a bowl and mix in the oil, cheese, and seasonings. Fill the pastry shells with the mixture.

Roll out the remaining pastry dough and make lids for the shells. Seal the lids with the beaten egg. Cut a small x in the middle of each lid. Bake in a preheated 400°F oven for 15–18 minutes until the pastry is golden. Serve warm.

CDW

Cheese Zebras with Parmesan Ice Cream

These little pumpernickel stacks are a Dutch recipe and go very well with the eighteenth-century Parmesan Ice, to form an interesting appetizer or even a savory course. The ice cream comes from the *Italian Confectioner*, published in 1791. I like savory ices, but they are something that only have their vestigial remains in the champagne or mint sorbets served as an intercourse palate cleanser.

¾ cup (1½ sticks) butter, softened
2 hard-boiled egg yolks, pressed through a sieve
1 teaspoon Worcestershire sauce
1½ cups grated mature Gouda cheese
salt and freshly ground pepper
4 slices pumpernickel bread

FOR THE PARMESAN ICE CREAM:
¼ cup sugar
1¼ cups water
6 eggs, beaten
2½ cups heavy cream
¾ cup grated Parmesan cheese

Cream the butter and add the egg yolks, Worcestershire sauce, cheese, and salt and pepper. Spread the mixture on the pumpernickel to the same thickness as the bread. Top with another slice of bread and repeat for two more layers. Cover with plastic wrap and chill for at least 2 hours.

To make the ice cream, dissolve the sugar in the water in a small pan over a low heat. Then boil rapidly without stirring, until the syrup reduces to 1¼ cups. Add the eggs and cream and heat slowly until the mixture thickens and comes to a boil. Stir in the cheese and pass through a strainer. Chill in the rerigerator, then freeze in an ice-cream maker or transfer to a shallow freezerproof container and place in the freezer. When the ice cream is almost frozen, remove from the freezer and mash with a fork, then refreeze until solid.

Cut the pumpernickel stacks into slices and serve with Parmesan Ice Cream.

CDW

Eggplants in Vinaigrette

This is another simple way to treat eggplants, that can be used as a salad, side dish, or what you will. It is also a very good accompaniment to cold pink lamb.

2 large eggplants
salt and freshly ground pepper
½ cup olive oil
2 garlic cloves, crushed
2 tablespoons lemon juice
1 tablespoon sugar
1 level teaspoon cumin
chopped parsley

Cut the eggplants into ½-inch thick slices, sprinkle with a little salt, and leave for 30 minutes. Wipe them dry with paper towels.

Brush the eggplant slices generously with olive oil, sprinkle with a little salt and pepper, and broil until the flesh is tender. Make a marinade of what's left of the olive oil, and the garlic, lemon juice, and cumin, mixing it well.

Put the slices of eggplant in a serving dish. Pour the marinade over, add a little salt and pepper, and sprinkle the parsley over. Leave for several hours before serving.

JP

Potted Turkey

This recipe is the best way I know of using up left over turkey. I invented it at a demonstration a year ago in Ireland and the only reason it wasn't in the last book was I forgot about it. It freezes beautifully, and is perfect as an appetizer with toast or for sandwiches.

1 cup (2 sticks) butter
1 garlic clove, crushed
6½ cups cooked turkey meat (both white and dark meat), cut into small pieces
juice of 1 lemon
1 scant teaspoon ground nutmeg
½ teaspoon cayenne pepper
salt and freshly ground pepper

In a heavy skillet, melt the butter and lightly fry the garlic. Throw in the turkey meat, add the lemon juice and all the seasonings, and stir well. Taste and adjust the seasoning. Put into a food processor and blend to a coarse paste. This will store well in the refrigerator or in a pot covered with a layer of clarified butter.

CDW

Spiced Pork Fillet

These little slices are a good thing to hand around with drinks to take the edge off the appetite. If used as an appetizer, dispense with the cocktails and eat them as you would salami, with the sauce on the side.

¼ cup soy sauce
1 garlic clove, crushed
2 shallots, finely chopped
2 tablespoons red wine
1 tablespoon honey
2 teaspoons brown sugar
1 teaspoon grated fresh gingerroot
¼ teaspoon ground cinnamon
1 pork tenderloin, trimmed of any sinew and fat
1 tablespoon olive oil

Combine all the ingredients, except the pork and oil, in a glass or ceramic bowl and mix them well. Place the pork tenderloin in this marinade and refrigerate for 3–4 hours, basting frequently, or leave it overnight.

When ready to cook, remove the pork and put it in an oiled roasting pan, reserving the marinade. Roast the pork in a preheated 350°F oven for about 45 minutes, turning and occasionally basting with the marinade to get an all-around roasting.

When cooked, leave to cool. Cut the pork into thin slices and use toothpicks for picking up the slices. If desired, strain the marinade, simmer it for 20 minutes, and cool then serve with the pork as a dipping sauce.

JP

Meat Patties in Horseradish Sauce

I was surprised when I saw fresh horseradish on sale in my local supermarket—well done to them. I grow a lot of horseradish, but always in a bucket or it takes over, just like mint. Grate the root in a food processor and you won't weep for days. The Scandinavians make much use of it, and this is a Swedish recipe. The Swedes are also fond of pickled beets but like it in a sweet pickle, not the harsh vinegar-based British variety.

Serves 6

2 medium onions, finely chopped
1 tablespoon butter
1 pound ground beefsteak
1 medium potato, boiled and mashed
8 ounces sweet pickled cooked beets, grated
1 egg, beaten
3 tablespoons milk
1 tablespoon capers, finely chopped
salt and freshly ground pepper
oil for frying

FOR THE SAUCE:
1 ¼ cups cream
salt
cayenne pepper
1 tablespoon freshly grated horseradish

Fry the onions in butter until soft and lightly brown. Mix them with the beef, potato, beets, egg, milk, capers, and seasoning until well combined. Shape into twelve patties and refrigerate for 1 hour. Combine the sauce ingredients.

Heat the oil in a large, heavy-bottomed pan and fry the patties for 5–10 minutes until they are cooked to your liking. I like to drain off any excess oil from the pan and pour it over the patties to heat them through before serving. In Sweden the sauce is served on the side of the plate.

CDW

The Butt and Ben's Arbroath Crêpes

Scotland's great legacy to food is cold smoking of fish, and, when it comes to haddock, ingenuity knows no bounds. There are at least sixty-nine recorded variants on the theme including some which are sun-dried, a patient version with Scots weather! Many know the Arbroath smokie, the famous smoked haddock, and because it is such an old product it is nice to think Robert I's stirring declaration of independence at Arbroath in 1320 might have been composed over a supper of them. What most people don't know, however, is that the Arbroath smokie originated along the coast to Authmithie and only moved when the trade became too large. If you go to Authmithie you must go to that excellent little restaurant the Butt and Ben. This delicious crêpe recipe is theirs.

FOR THE CRÊPE BATTER:
¾ cup plus 1 tablespoon all-purpose flour
pinch of salt
pinch of baking powder
1 egg
⅔ cup milk

FOR THE FILLING:
1 pair of Arbroath smokies or other smoked haddock
4 tablespoons (½ stick) butter
1¼ cups heavy cream

To make the crêpe batter, sift the flour, salt and baking powder into a bowl and make a well in the centre. Add the egg and whisk well. Gradually beat in the milk, drawing in the flour from the sides to make a smooth batter. Cover and leave the batter to stand for at least 1 hour.

Strip the skin from the smokies and flake the meat. Melt the butter with the cream in a pan and bring to just below the boiling point. Throw in the flaked smokies and heat through.

Make four crêpes with the batter. Heat the minimum amount of oil in a skillet and pour in just enough batter to thinly coat the base of the pan. Cook over a high heat for about 1 minute until golden brown. Turn or toss the crêpe and cook the other side for a further minute.

Divide the smokie mixture equally between the four crêpes, fold them over, and pour over any remaining sauce. Serve on hot plates.

CDW

Smoked Trout, Avocado, and Shrimp Mousse

This is a very 1960s type of mousse, when the thrill of the avocado had just about reached us in England. However, it is always very good and I like to eat it with hot wheat toast and a squeeze of lemon on the side.

2 8–10-ounce smoked trout fillets

1 ripe avocado

1¼ cups crème fraîche

juice of ½ lemon

2 tablespoons finely grated lemon zest

6 ounces cooked and shelled shrimp

salt and freshly ground black pepper

Skin and bone the trout. Peel and pit the avocado. Put both in a blender or food processor and purée. Add the crème fraîche, lemon juice, lemon zest, and salt and pepper and blend again. Place half the mixture in a ceramic soufflé dish, cover with a layer of shrimp and then with the remaining mixture. Chill the mousse well before serving.

JP

Illustrated overleaf

Soused Herring

The herring is probably one of the cheapest fish you can buy. It is also extremely good for you, providing essential oils. These soused herring, probably originating in Denmark, make a good hors d'œuvre, which is improved by a dollop of sour cream.

4 herrings, dressed and boned
1 small onion, sliced
1 tablespoon mixed pickling spice
2 bay leaves
salt and freshly ground pepper
⅔ cup dry white wine
⅔ cup good wine vinegar

Lay the herrings in a baking dish, cover with the onion, sprinkle with the pickling spices, and add the bay leaves, and salt and pepper. Mix the wine and wine vinegar together and pour over.

Cook in a preheated 300°F oven for about 1½ hours. Allow to cool completely before serving.

JP

Salmon Mousse with Cucumber Sauce

The use of blue cheese in this mousse means it will lift even the blandest of farmed salmon. Clearly you don't want to use expensive wild salmon for this dish, but use a good-quality farmed one. I cooked it for the barristers in the Lincoln's Inn program and it was much admired. You can use any size mold, from small individual ones for a first course to very large ones for a buffet. If you don't overcook the fish or mess up with your gelatin, this recipe is foolproof.

1-pound salmon fillet
4 tablespoons (½ stick) butter, melted
salt and freshly ground pepper
2 ounces blue cheese
½ cup cream cheese
½ cup sour cream
2 gerkins, finely chopped
1 envelop unflavored gelatin
1 celery stalk, chopped
1 medium onion, finely chopped
1¼ cups whipping cream, whipped
1 tablespoon chopped dill
juice of ½ lemon

FOR THE SAUCE:
1 cucumber
1 tablespoon chopped chives
½ teaspoon sugar
1 tablespoon white vinegar
⅔ cup sour cream

Clean and skin the salmon and place it into a buttered baking dish, add the melted butter and season with salt and pepper. Cover and bake in a preheated 350°F oven for 15-20 minutes.

Skin, bone, and flake the salmon into a large mixing bowl. Mix the cheeses and the sour cream together, combine with the salmon and add the gerkins. Dissolve the gelatin in water following the packet directions and blend into the salmon mixture. Add the remaining ingredients and mix well. Pour into wetted molds and refrigerate for at least 2 hours, or until set.

To make the sauce, peel, seed, and finely chop the cucumber. Mix with all the remaining ingredients, except the sour cream, and leave for 30 minutes. Strain off the liquid and mix with the sour cream. Unmold the mousse and serve with the sauce.

CDW

Salmon Terrine

A salmon terrine is always a good thing to have up your sleeve in case unexpected guests arrive, especially on a Sunday after cocktails. Easy to make, it can be left in the refrigerator ready to pounce on when necessary.

1½ pounds raw salmon, boned and skinned
2 tablespoons chopped shallot
salt and freshly ground pepper
¼ cup dry white wine
½ pound whiting or any white fish, dressed, boned and skinned
1½ cups fresh bread crumbs, soaked in milk and squeezed dry
6 tablespoons (¾ stick) butter, softened
1 tablespoon chopped parsley
2 teaspoons chopped chives
¼ teaspoon ground nutmeg
1 whole egg and 2 egg yolks, beaten

Cut 1 pound of the salmon into finger-size pieces and place in a glass dish. Sprinkle with the shallot, salt and pepper to taste, and white wine. Place the rest of the salmon, the white fish, and bread crumbs in a food processor and blend together. Add 4 tablespoons (½ stick) of the butter, the parsley, chives, and nutmeg and bind the whole lot together with the beaten eggs.

Butter a six cup terrine with the remaining butter. Put a layer of the crumb mixture on the bottom, cover with a layer of salmon fingers, add more crumb mixture and continue in this fashion until the ingredients are finished. Strain the marinade onto the terrine, and put the lid on the terrine. Cook in a bain marie in a preheated 325°F oven for 1½–2 hours. Cool completely before serving.

JP

Rabbit Pâté

For all that is talked about lean meat, rabbit is still scorned and the wastage of this good and healthy meat every year is immense. I like a delicate rabbit pâté much better than a chicken one—the flavor is real and it is a lot safer.

2 pounds rabbit meat
2 pounds boneless pork
1 pound bacon
2 onions, peeled
1 tablespoon finely chopped parsley
2 teaspoons thyme
3 liqueur glasses brandy
salt and freshly ground pepper
bottle of cornichons (small gerkins)
1 bay leaf
½ pound thin slices of bacon

Coarsely grind or process the rabbit, pork, bacon, and onions together. Add the other ingredients, except the cornichons, bay leaf, and bacon slices, and mix, using your hands, until they are all well amalgamated.

Half fill an eight cup earthenware terrine with the rabbit mixture, then put in a double layer of cornichons. Fill to the top with more mixture, place the bay leaf on top, cover with bacon slices cut into thin strips, and press down well. Add a layer of aluminum foil.

Cover and cook in a bain marie in a preheated 300°F oven for 1 hour for small terrines, or 2 hours if large. To store, pour over a layer of melted vegetable shortening and cover with a piece of waxed paper. Store in a cool place for a month or more.

CDW

FISH AND SHELLFISH

The ladies receive some direction at Kylemore Abbey in western Ireland, with the Mother Abbess looking on.

CLARISSA WRITES: I am tempted to say unless you have a good fish merchant don't bother. As Jennifer says, if it smells of fish it isn't fresh. Moreover, you can talk to your fish merchant: I have been in pursuit of gulls' eggs since the year began and my own dear Mr. Clarke found them for me. When I went to collect them he was extolling the virtues of an 11-stone (154-pound) halibut caught off the west coast, so I bought some of that too. This set me thinking. When I was young a fish that size was the norm—turbot were huge monsters and a cod was a denizen of the depths, but nowadays overfishing has destroyed all that. A Hong Kong lawyer was telling me recently that the waters around Asia are all fished out, and Mr. Doyle, owner of Sydney's most famous seafood restaurant, had been on television predicting a day when Australians would no longer be able to afford to buy their own seafood because of the Asian Maw. It makes me think that supermarkets should be banned from selling what they don't know how to look after properly, and mass-produced frozen fish concoctions should be banned too, to prevent waste of this diminishing asset.

I like to serve a separate fish course at a dinner party but most people will have it as a main course. It is a good choice if you are eating late as it is easily digestible and takes no time to cook. Filming at a convent in Galway on the

Taking a break from all that cooking.

west coast of Ireland took me back to my child-hood, when I used to visit cousins on the Donegal coast. We would fish for mackerel from an old dinghy, and how good they tasted fresh from the sea. So too did the fish we caught from the line trailed behind the Caribbean yacht I worked on, hauling them into the boat in a hurry before the sharks could get at them. Nowhere in Great Britain is far from the sea, and yet you find fresher fish in the hill towns of inland Spain than we can. In this age of activists I wish you would all go out and protest for fresher, safer products rather than just not buying what is available.

The trick with fish is to make your guests wait for it rather than the other way around. I never understand people who want everything cooked before people arrive—some of my most pleasant dalliances have been conducted in my kitchen during a dinner party! And anyway I'm not that keen on casseroles. In this age of fisharians (i.e. vegetarians who eat fish) the ability to cook it well is of great importance. We are always being

told how good oily fish is for us and eating it is so much nicer than swallowing a spoonful of cod liver oil. It is also important to try the different range of fish available. So many people just stick to cod, haddock, or salmon, but don't be afraid to experiment and ask your fish merchant what is particularly good or in season—remember fish have seasons, just like fruit and vegetables.

In Connemara, Jennifer cooked lobster and we had great fun tracking the local lobster king from the quay to the pub, as one might expect in Ireland. We found him sitting happily quaffing his Guinness with a wooden box containing six live lobsters by his side. They were beautiful lobsters and the nuns did them justice, but sadly the ones we ate in our hotel were overcooked, and overcooked fish is a sin against heaven.

In the grounds of Kylemore Abbey, with a tranquil view over the water.

Fish Stew

You can use any fish in this recipe but I favor the fleshier ones such as monkfish, coley, and red mullet, which all give a good flavor. Ask your fish merchant to fillet and clean them. If you like, add spoonfuls of aïoli to the finished stew, once in the bowl.

1 large onion, chopped
1 large leek, white part only, cleaned and chopped
2 celery stalks, fibers removed and chopped
2 garlic cloves, finely chopped
2 cups finely sliced mushrooms
2 potatoes, peeled and chopped
1 tablespoon olive oil
2 tablespoons (¼ stick) butter
3 large tomatoes, skinned and chopped
1½ pounds assorted fish, cut into chunks
⅔ cup white wine
1¼ cups water
1 bouquet garni
2 bay leaves
salt and freshly ground pepper
1 tablespoon chopped parsley
pinch of saffron

Fry the onion, leek, celery, garlic, mushrooms, and potatoes in the oil and butter until the onion begins to brown. Add the chopped tomatoes. Add the fish and cover with the wine and water. Add the bouquet garni, bay leaves, and salt and pepper to taste.

Bring to a boil and simmer for 12–15 minutes. Add the parsley and the saffron before serving.

JP

Fish with Egg and Lemon Sauce

This is a very comforting dish with the traditional Greek avoglemoni sauce. If you can't go to my fishmonger, Mr. Clarke, find one nearby and make a friend of him and then you can be sure of getting really fresh fish. It will be better than the ammoniac stuff which you follow your nose to in some supermarkets.

2–3 celery stalks or equivalent celery root
3 tablespoons olive oil
2 tablespoons (¼ stick) butter
1 small onion, finely sliced
¼ cup white wine
⅔ cup water
4 fish steaks

FOR THE SAUCE:
2 egg yolks
juice of 1 lemon

chopped dill or parsley
salt and freshly ground pepper

Poach the celery or celery root in boiling salted water for 4 minutes. Drain. Heat the olive oil and butter in a heavy-bottomed pan and sauté the onion until gilded but not brown. Add the wine and the water and bring to a boil. Add the celery and mix well. Cover and cook gently for 5 minutes.

Add the fish and spoon the mixture over. The fish should be half immersed in the liquid; if not add a little more water. Cover and simmer gently for about 10–15 minutes, until the fish feels tender but is not overcooked. Remove from the heat and keep warm. Let it stand for 5 minutes while you make the sauce.

Using a fork, beat the egg yolks with a tablespoon of water for 2 minutes. Add the lemon juice and beat for a further minute. Add 4–5 tablespoons of juice from the fish (a tablespoon at a time), stirring well with a wooden spoon. Pour the sauce over the fish and shake the saucepan well to distribute. Sprinkle with dill or parsley, season to taste and return to a very low heat for 2–3 minutes, stirring gently until the sauce thickens, taking care not to break the fish. Serve with new potatoes and a green salad.

CDW

Cod Fillet in Mushroom, Shrimp, and Cheese Sauce

Far from being the cheapest fish as it was not so many years ago, cod has now reached its rightful place on the menus of every grand restaurant.

½ cup (1 stick) butter
5 tablespoons all-purpose flour
4 thick cod fillets
1¼ cups fish stock
1¼ cups milk
1½ cups mushrooms, halved
¾ cup grated sharp cheddar cheese
1 teaspoon anchovy extract or anchovy paste
salt and freshly ground pepper
½ pound small cooked shrimp, shelled
1 tablespoon chopped parsley

Melt 4 tablespoons of the butter in a saucepan. Add the flour, stir, and allow to bubble for 2–3 minutes, but be careful not to let it burn. Remove from the heat. Butter a flameproof dish with 1 tablespoon of the remaining butter and place the cod fillets in it, cover with the fish stock and cook in a preheated 375°F oven for 15 minutes. Strain off the fish stock, add to the milk, and gradually stir this into the saucepan containing the flour and butter. Bring slowly to a boil, stirring gently, to get a smooth consistency.

Sauté the mushrooms in the remaining butter. Add to your sauce with ¼ cup of the cheese and the anchovy extract or paste. Stir until the cheese melts, and season to taste.

Cut the fish into bite-size pieces. Add the shrimp and parsley to the fish in the baking dish, and pour the sauce over the fish, shaking the dish gently for the sauce to sink. Place the dish in a preheated 400°F oven for 10 minutes. Sprinkle the remaining cheese over and put the dish under a hot broiler for a few minutes for the cheese to melt and brown.

JP

Smoked Haddock and Lovage Tart

This recipe comes from *Feasting on Herbs,* an excellent book by my dear friend Sue Lawrence, who is one of the best cooks I know. I cooked it untested for a dinner of Gaelic poets and it was much praised by the late great Sorley Maclean. As he was speaking Gaelic at the time I can't tell you what he said. It is excellent, and I know you will love it.

FOR THE PASTRY DOUGH:
1 cup plus 1 tablespoon all-purpose flour
½ cup plus 1 tablespoon polenta
salt
½ cup (1 stick) unsalted butter
1 egg, lightly beaten
1 tablespoon olive oil

FOR THE FILLING:
12 ounces undyed smoked haddock
⅔ cup milk
⅔ cup light cream
3 eggs
2 tablespoons chopped fresh lovage
salt and freshly ground pepper

To make your pastry in a food processor, mix all the dried ingredients, chop in the butter, add the egg and oil, spinning until a paste forms. Chill for 30 minutes. Roll out and line a 9-inch tart pan with a removeable bottom. The pastry will be very crumbly so patch it in by hand and chill in the pan for a further 30 minutes. Line the pastry with baking paper and dried beans. Bake in a preheated 375°F oven until the pastry is cooked and pale gold, 15–20 minutes. Cool slightly, but do not turn off the oven.

Meanwhile, poach the fish in the milk. Remove from milk and flake the flesh into the piecrust, reserving the milk. Whisk the cream and eggs into the reserved milk and add the lovage. Season and pour over the fish. Return to the oven and bake for 30 minutes, or until the filling is set. Cool slightly before serving. This is also good cold.

CDW

Hake Portuguese

Both the Portuguese and the Spanish have a passion for hake. It is a very good fish although not used much by the British—pray go out and buy some. It is also very good cold, covered in mayonnaise, and served with a beautiful potato salad.

½ cup (1 stick) butter
2 tablespoons olive oil
8 shallots, finely chopped
4 ½-pound cuts of hake
1 pound tomatoes, skinned, seeded, and chopped
1 yellow bell pepper, skinned, seeded, and chopped
1 tablespoon frozen peas
¾ cup cooked (al dente) rice
2 tablespoons chopped parsley
2 glasses white wine
salt and freshly ground pepper

Melt 2 tablespoons (¼ stick) of the butter with the olive oil in a flameproof dish. Add the shallots and fry until they are translucent. Lay the fish on top of the cooked shallots and dot with knobs of the remaining butter. Cover the fish with chopped tomatoes, yellow bell pepper, and frozen peas. Surround the fish with the rice and chopped parsley. Pour in the wine, and add salt and pepper. Bake in a 375°F oven for 30–35 minutes.

JP

Halibut Burgers with Anchovy Aïoli

This is another Swedish dish and a good use for the excellent halibut coming onto the market. My Mr. Clarke gets it line-caught from the Orkneys, although just recently he has been getting some good fish from the Firth of Forth, which is good news for Edinburghers. If you don't like the Swedish version of aïoli make it the ordinary way.

FOR THE AÏOLI:
3 small potatoes, peeled
3 egg yolks
¾ cup olive oil
1 garlic clove, minced
5 anchovy fillets, chopped

1½-pound halibut fillet
salt and freshly ground pepper
4 tablespoons (½ stick) butter
8 slices country bread
tomato relish
1 red onion, sliced

To make the aïoli, boil and mash the potatoes. Cool and combine with the egg yolks. Add the olive oil in a thin stream a few drops at a time, whisking all the time until all the oil is mixed in. Mix the garlic and anchovies into the aïoli.

Divide the fish into four pieces, season with salt and pepper, and fry in the butter for about 1 minute on each side. Toast the bread and smear with tomato relish. Put a piece of fish on top of a piece of bread, dab with some aïoli, then place a slice of red onion on top and finish with another slice of bread.

CDW

Singapore Shrimp with Bugis Street Sauce

I haven't been back to Singapore since 1948 but I always remember these marvelous shrimp dishes I had in Bugis Street. This recipe is the nearest I can get to one of the sauces. There was always a side dish of small red chilies and one of our friends would chew these as if he was eating peanuts. The more reserved of us would take one or two.

2 tablespoons vegetable oil
1½ cups sliced mushrooms
¼ cup chopped scallions
1 garlic clove, chopped
1 teaspoon grated fresh gingerroot
1½ tablespoons hoisin sauce
1½ tablespoons oyster sauce
2 teaspoons red Thai curry paste
pinch of five-spice powder
1¼ cups coconut milk
salt and freshly ground pepper
1½ pounds cooked and shelled small shrimp

Heat the vegetable oil in wok or skillet. Add the mushrooms, scallions, garlic, and ginger and stir fry for a couple of minutes. Add the hoisin sauce, oyster sauce, red curry paste, and five-spice powder and stir well. Then add the coconut milk, a little salt and pepper, and the shrimp and simmer gently for 1–2 minutes. Serve on a bed of rice or noodles.

JP

Caper-Stuffed Herring with Warm Potato Salad

I have no time for people who purport to listen to the health pundits and then eat cod-liver oil capsules as their answer to oily fish. I love herrings—the food history of our coastal areas is ripe with herring stories and accounts of the indomitable herring wives who followed the shoals of fish around the country. This is a Swedish dish and an excellent way of cooking your herring.

⅓ cup drained capers
2 tablespoons chopped chives
2 tablespoons dill
1 tablespoon freshly grated horseradish
3 ounces cream cheese
6 herrings, butterflied and boned but still connected along the back fin
salt and freshly ground pepper

FOR THE SALAD:
7 slices of bacon, chopped
6 cold, boiled small potatoes, roughly chopped
2 shallots or 1 small onion, finely chopped
wine vinegar
olive oil

1 tablespoon drained capers

Chop the capers and mix with the chives, dill, and horseradish. Add the cream cheese and season to taste. Dry the fish, lay the filling on one side and fold over so the fish looks whole.

Fry the bacon in a heavy pan until crisp. Add the potatoes and heat through, remove to a dish, and stir in the shallots or onion. Pour over the vinegar and a little olive oil, season, and mix well. Keep warm.

Rub the fish with a little oil and heat the pan; it must be very hot. Fry the fish for about 2 minutes on each side. Serve with the potato salad, garnished with capers.

CDW

Monkfish and Baked Potato Kebabs

This is a quirky kebab, but one I think you will enjoy. We have talked before of gigot of monkfish, so why not a kebab!

2 large potatoes
salt and freshly ground pepper
1 tablespoon oil
1 pound trimmed monkfish fillet
2 tablespoons olive oil
2 tablespoons (¼ stick) butter
juice of ½ lemon
½ cup grated sharp cheddar cheese
6 tablespoons sour cream

Rub the potatoes with salt and oil and bake for 1 hour in a pre-heated 425°F oven.

Cut the monkfish into 1-inch chunks. Heat the olive oil and butter and sauté the fish until just cooked through, about 5 minutes. Season with lemon juice. Slice the potatoes carefully crosswise to leave each piece intact. Thread alternate pieces of fish and potato on pre-soaked wooden or metal skewers and place in a flameproof dish.

Mix together the cheese and the sour cream and season. Ladle over the kebabs and sear under a very hot broiler until the cheese bubbles. Serve at once.

CDW

Coconut Salmon

This is a dish I invented when demonstrating at the Highland Show with the mad boys from Herbie's Delicatessen in Edinburgh. I happened to have a lot of creamed coconut in my pantry and thought it would be an interesting experiment. I was delighted with the result.

3 ounces creamed coconut (available from Asian food stores)
⅔ cup hot water
1 shallot, finely chopped
1 garlic clove, finely chopped
½-inch fresh gingerroot, finely chopped
½ teaspoon ground cardamom
½ teaspoon ground cumin
salt and freshly ground pepper
4 salmon fillets, skinned

Dissolve the coconut in the hot water and add the shallot, garlic, and ginger. Rub the cardamom, cumin, and black pepper into the salmon fillets and set aside for at least 30 minutes.

Pour the coconut mixture into a sauté pan and simmer until reduced by half. Add salt to taste and the salmon fillets, turning to coat with sauce. Cook for 6–8 minutes and serve.

CDW

Salmon Fillets with Leeks and Cream

This is a good idea for using farmed salmon, which is cheaper than the wild but can do with extra flavoring. The leeks go well with the fish without overpowering it. Very suitable for a visiting maiden aunt, of which I am one.

½ cup (1 stick) butter
4 medium-size leeks, cleaned and finely chopped
4 4-ounce salmon fillets
1¼ cups heavy cream, lightly whipped
½ pound cooked and shelled shrimp
juice of ½ lemon
salt and pepper
tin foil

Melt 6 tablespoons (¾ stick) of the butter in a skillet. Add the leeks and sauté over low heat until soft.

Smear four sheets of aluminum foil large enough to loosely enclose one fillet and one-quarter of the leeks with the remaining butter.

Place a generous layer of leek in the center of each foil sheet, add a salmon fillet, another layer of leek and top with a generous dollop of cream and one-quarter of the shrimp. Sprinkle about 1 teaspoon of lemon juice over the top of each. Bring the edges of the foil together and make into a parcel so none of the juices run out.

Place the parcels on a baking sheet and cook in a preheated 375°F oven for 25 minutes.

JP

Salmon in Red Pepper Sauce

You all know how to peel bell peppers, I'm sure—char them over a flame or under a broiler, put them immediately in a plastic bag and allow them to cool, and the skin slides off easily. Do not make the mistake a well-known cookery writer once made, in front of a large audience, of trying to peel them straight from the flame. She was unable to do a book signing for me as we had no gloves to cover the ointment. The egg white gives a bit more body to the sauce.

2 red bell peppers
2 garlic cloves
salt and freshly ground pepper
1 egg white
2 pound fillet of salmon
1 cup fish stock
1 cup red wine

Char and peel the peppers. Place in a blender or food processor, purée them with the garlic cloves and a pinch of salt until smooth. Add the egg white and process again.

Season the salmon and place in a fish kettle or large saucepan, add enough of the stock and wine to cover the fish, replace the lid and poach the fish for about 30 minutes. Remove the fish, reduce the stock by about half and add the red pepper mixture. Heat through gently and serve with the fish.

CDW

Roasted Salmon with Scallops and Mustard Butter

I can't tell you how good this is. I was introduced to it by Guy Harrington, one of our dear researchers, who in his day ran many a restaurant or strummed the piano in far-off bars. We had it as an appetizer, but it could be a splendid main course with a few new potatoes.

2-pound middle cut piece of salmon, boned, or fillets
¾ cup (1½ sticks) butter
3 generous teaspoons wholegrain mustard
4 level teaspoons dried dillweed, or 2 teaspoons each dried and fresh dill
salt and freshly ground pepper
8 sea scallops
10 ounces fresh spinach or arugula

Place the salmon piece or fillets skin-side up in a shallow baking dish. Roast in a preheated 450°F oven for 15 minutes.

Meanwhile, gently melt the butter in a small saucepan. Remove from the heat and stir in the mustard and dill. Season to taste.

Remove the salmon from the oven, place the scallops around it, and baste with the mustard sauce. Return to the oven for a further 5 minutes.

Slice the salmon quite thickly, serve on top of the spinach or arugula and spoon over the mustard butter.

JP

Illustrated overleaf

Squash Stuffed with Salmon

This dish was inspired by a letter from my Hungarian barrister friend John Zeigler, who wrote to admonish me on my misrepresentation of Rigo Jancsi chocolate slices. In the letter he referred to a Hungarian way of serving marrow squash with salmon. This isn't it, but it is a fun dish all the same.

Serves 2-3

½-pound salmon fillet
salt and freshly ground pepper
⅓ cup cooked rice
1 tablespoon chopped pickled
cucumber
1 tablespoon sour cream
1 tablespoon chopped dill
1 medium marrow squash or
very large zucchini
2 tablespoons (¼ stick) butter,
melted

In a skillet, briefly sauté the salmon until you can flake it. Season well. Mix the salmon with the other ingredients, except the marrow squash or zucchini and the butter.

Cut a cap from the broad end of the squash and hollow out, removing the seeds and some flesh. Rub the inside with pepper. Stuff with the filling. Replace the cap and secure with some foil.

Place in a baking dish, brush with butter, cover with aluminum foil, and bake in a preheated 350°F oven for 1–1½ hours.

CDW

Baked Stuffed Sewin

Sewin may be more familiar to you by one of its other names: sea trout, salmon trout, or brown trout to name just a few. To my mind it is even better than salmon. It is a good natural fish with a delicate flavor which can be bought in different sizes according to need. It is very good plain with a sauce verte, but this recipe is a little more exciting and has my beloved anchovy fillets within.

4 1-pound sewin
½ cup fresh white bread crumbs
⅔ cup milk
1 cup shallots, finely chopped
6 mushrooms, stems removed and chopped small
¾ cup (1½ sticks) butter
1 egg
2 tablespoons chopped parsley
juice of ½ lemon
pinch of grated nutmeg
salt and freshly ground pepper
4 anchovy fillets, soaked in milk for 30 minutes

Ask your fish merchant to remove the bones from the sewin, but leave the fish whole. Soak the bread crumbs in the milk, then squeeze out the bread crumbs and set aside.

Gently fry the shallots and mushrooms in ½ cup (1 stick) of the butter, until the shallots become translucent.

Mix the bread crumbs with the egg, chopped parsley, lemon juice, grated nutmeg, and salt and pepper. Add to the mushroom mixture. Stuff a quarter of the mixture into the cavity of each fish, and add an anchovy fillet to each one. Wrap each fish in aluminum foil.

Grease a baking dish with the rest of the butter, and add the foil-wrapped fish. Bake in a preheated 375°F oven for 40 minutes.

JP

Lobster with Latkas

I have an unlimited passion for lobsters, which I do very well with, thanks to my dear Mr. Clarke of Fisher Row, Musselburgh, the best fishmonger in Britain. I also love latkas, those crispy mouthwatering Jewish potato pancakes. So it seemed to me an excellent idea to combine the two.

4 boiled lobsters (see page 64)
6 tablespoons (¾ stick) butter
scant 1 cup sliced shallots
2 cups sliced mushrooms
⅔ cup whiskey
freshly ground black pepper
pinch of ground cloves
1¼ cups heavy cream

FOR THE LATKAS:
2 pounds potatoes, peeled and finely grated
1½ cups grated onion
1½ cups matzo meal (use flour if not available)
4 eggs
2 teaspoons caraway seeds
salt and freshly ground pepper
oil for shallow frying

Remove the meat from the lobsters and cut into pieces. Melt 4 tablespoons (½ stick) of the butter in a skillet and fry the shallots until soft. Add the mushrooms and cook gently until soft, add the lobster, and mix well. Cover and cook very slowly for 3 minutes. Warm the whiskey, set it alight and, when the flames have died down, pour over the lobster. Season with black pepper and cloves and stir in the cream. Shake over the heat until well mixed, cover, and cook over a very low heat for 5 minutes.

To make the latkas, rinse the grated potatoes in several changes of cold water to remove excess starch. Pat dry with a towel and mix with the rest of the ingredients, except the oil. Season well.

Heat enough to shallow fry the latkas in a large skillet. Drop tablespoons of the mixture into the hot oil, flatten each dollop into a round, small flat pancake, and fry over a medium heat for 3–4 minutes on each side until the pancake is a pale golden brown and perfectly crisp. Drain on paper towels and serve very hot with the lobster. If you are being stylish you can stack the latkas with lobster sandwiched between and the sauce drizzled around the base of the stack.

CDW

Lobster with Mayonnaise

When making the mayonnaise, it is essential all the ingredients are at room temperature. The eggs should not be stored in the refrigerator because they will curdle when making the mayonnaise.

1 lobster per serving

FOR 1¼ CUPS OF MAYONNAISE:
2 egg yolks
1 level teaspoon Dijon mustard
salt and freshly ground black pepper
lemon juice or white wine vinegar, according to taste
1¼ cups olive oil, sunflower oil, or a mixture of the two

Fill a pan with lukewarm water and place it on a high heat. Place the lobsters in the pan and cover. Once the water has come to the boil, cook the lobsters for 10 minutes, or until they no longer have any blue hue and turn a deep red-orange color.

Remove the lobsters from the pan and leave to cool. Once cool you can prepare the lobster in the traditional manner: using a sharp knife, make an incision at the point where the head joins the body and cut down the length of the lobster toward the tail. Make sure you cut all the way through the body. Now turn the lobster 180 degrees and cut from the original incision back through the head. With your fingers gradually prise the shell apart so it falls into halves. Remove the front claws and set aside. With your index finger, prise the meat out of the shell (trying to keep it in one piece, again working from the tail upward). Replace the meat in the shell (this process makes it easier for your guests to keep their fingers clean) and repeat with the second half. Using a cleaver or hammer, crack both sides of the claws. Remove the surrounding shell and extract the meat in a single piece. Arrange two lobster halves on each plate together with the claw meat and serve with mayonnaise.

To make the mayonnaise put the eggs, mustard, a pinch of salt, a grinding of pepper and a small squeeze of lemon juice or vinegar in a bowl and beat well with a wooden spoon or whisk. Start adding the oil, drop by drop to begin with, stirring all the time. When the mixture starts to emulsify you may add more oil in steady dribblets but keep stirring until you get the required jelly-like substance, which is the consistency that proper mayonnaise should be. Finally test for more seasoning.

JP

Baked Sole with Horseradish

I love horseradish and clearly from the way old plantings of it still grow around ancient dwellings it was once more generally used. It is an excellent digestive, but in British cooking its use really only survives with beef, whereas in Scandinavia and Central Europe it is used much more extensively. This is a Polish recipe given to me by an old lady in whose Sussex lake we used to fish as children.

8 sole, flounder or haddock fillets
salt
1 tablespoon white-wine vinegar
2 tablespoons (½ stick) butter, melted
4 ounces horseradish, grated
1 tart apple, peeled, cored, and shredded
¾ cup sour cream
sugar

Sprinkle the fish with salt and vinegar. Place in a buttered baking dish and drizzle with melted butter. Bake in a preheated 400°F oven for 10 minutes.

Mix the horseradish, apple, and sour cream together. Season with salt and sugar. Pour this mixture over the fish and bake for a further 10 minutes. Serve with boiled potatoes.

CDW

Sole in Vermouth

Vermouth is always good with fish, having a stronger flavor than any white wine and, as I'm not tempted to drink it on its own, I always seem to have some. Sole is one of the finest fish, but alas now very expensive. However, we all deserve a great treat every now and then. So enjoy.

3 shallots, finely chopped
¾ cup (1½ sticks) butter
2 tablespoons finely chopped parsley
1 tablespoon fresh tarragon
8 sole fillets
salt and freshly ground pepper
dry vermouth
juice of ½ lemon

Soften the shallots in 4 tablespoons (½ stick) of the butter in a large flameproof dish. Add the parsley and tarragon. Place the fish fillets on top of shallots and herbs, and season with salt and pepper. Pour in sufficient vermouth to come level with the fish. Dot the fish with 4 tablespoons (½ stick) of the remaining butter. Cook in a preheated 425°F oven for 20–30 minutes, or until the fish flakes easily.

Remove the fish to a hot serving dish. Pour the juices into a saucepan and boil to reduce rapidly by half. Remove the pan from the heat and whisk in the remaining butter. Taste for seasoning, add a squeeze of lemon juice, and pour the sauce over fish.

JP

Trout with Olives, Orange, Tomato, and Vermouth

I originally invented this dish to go with pheasant, but people kept bringing me trout so I thought I'd give it a try and it works equally well with either. Men who shoot often fish as well, so the versatility will be appreciated by those who have to handle the spoils!

4 slices of bacon, chopped
12 shallots
4 tablespoons (½ stick) butter
5 trout, cleaned and gutted
salt and freshly ground pepper
12 black olives
4 green olives
¼ cup stock
½ cup vermouth
juice of 1 orange
¾ cup tomato juice

Sauté the bacon and shallots in the butter. Add the trout, season well, and cook for 2½ minutes on each side. Add the olives, stock, vermouth, and orange and tomato juices and cook till done, about 10 minutes.

CDW

Trout in Rosé de Loire

A lovely pink trout with a lovely pink sauce. A very suitable dish for mid-Lent or a mid-Advent Sunday when Church of England priests always wear pink vestments.

4 medium-size trout, cleaned, gutted, and boned
½ cup (1 stick) butter
4 shallots, chopped
2½ cups Rosé de Loire
1 bouquet garni
salt and freshly ground pepper
4 egg yolks
¼ cup heavy cream
1 tablespoon pink lumpfish roe
¼ cup croutons

Ask your fish merchant to gut and bone the trout. Melt 4 tablespoons of the butter in a skillet and gently sauté the shallots, until golden but not brown. Add the trout and cook gently on both sides until lightly brown all over.

Butter a baking dish with half the remaining butter. Place the trout in the dish, add the wine, bouquet garni, and salt and pepper. Dot each fish with knobs of the remaining butter. Cook in a preheated 350°F oven for 25–30 minutes, basting once or twice. Place the fish on a serving plate and keep warm.

Pour the residual juices into a small saucepan and boil rapidly until reduced by half. Allow to cool for 2 minutes. Whisk the egg yolks with the cream and slowly add the juices while continuing to whisk. When the mixture is light and frothy, pour it over the fish. Serve immediately, garnished with lumpfish roe and croutons.

JP

Trout Quenelles with Watercress Sauce

Although, as my friend Angus quite rightly, if somewhat acerbically, pointed out, the French only use pike when making quenelles, trout is an excellent substitute. I served trout quenelles at a ten-course dinner party I once cooked in an alcoholic blackout, so you can see this recipe is not difficult.

10 ounces boneless fresh trout
10 ounces boneless smoked trout
3 egg whites
salt and freshly ground pepper
a pinch of ground mace
1¼ cups heavy cream

FOR THE SAUCE:
5 tablespoons finely chopped shallot
⅔ cup dry white wine
⅔ cup strong chicken stock
1¼ cups whipping cream
4 bunches watercress
lemon juice, to taste
4 tablespoons (½ stick) butter, cut into small pieces

Put all the fish into a food processor and blend until smooth. Add the egg whites and blend again until completely smooth. Add the mace, salt and pepper, and pour in the cream with the machine running. Do not run the machine for more than 20 seconds or the mixture wil become too thin; it must sit up on a spoon. Chill for 30 minutes.

Bring a wide pan of salted water to a simmer. Dip a dessert spoon in warm water and take a good rounded spoonful of the trout mixture. Use another spoon to form the quenelle. Poach the quenelle in the water for 8–10 minutes, remove with a slotted spoon and drain on paper towels. Put in a warm dish and repeat with the remaining trout mixture. When all the quenelles are made, reheat the sauce without boiling, pour over the quenelles, and serve at once.

To make the sauce, simmer the shallot and the wine together for 15 minutes or more until they form a soft purée and the wine is almost evaporated. Add the stock and cream, season, and boil until reduced by one-third and thick enough to coat a spoon. Pick over the watercress, discarding tough stems and discolored leaves. Toss the leaves into a pan of boiling salted water and blanch for 2–3 minutes. Drain and refresh under cold water. Squeeze out any excess water. Purée the watercress in a blender for 1–2 minutes until a smooth purée forms. Pour the reduced cream mixture over the purée and process, adding the lemon juice and butter. Strain.

CDW

Fresh Tuna Salad

During a shoot we tend to eat rather a lot and rather late. There is nothing I like more on my return to my flat in London than a simple salade Niçoise. I always feel there is something very restorative about it.

1 tuna steak per person, about 1 inch thick
12 ounces baby new potatoes
4 tablespoons (½ stick) salted butter
3 garlic cloves
4–5 tablespoons olive oil
2 tablespoons chopped chervil
salt and pepper
2 tablespoons balsamic vinegar
4 ounces green beans
½ pound cherry tomatoes
1 red onion, thickly sliced
10 lettuce leaves—Romaine or similar
3 hard-boiled eggs, shelled and quartered
8 anchovy fillets
12 black olives

You can broil the tuna but it is far better cooked on a ridged, cast-iron griddle, turned both ways to achieve a crisscross pattern. Broil or grill the tuna for about 1½ minutes in total, so it is still pink in the middle. If you prefer it well done, cook for 1½ minutes on each side.

Par-boil the potatoes, and then sauté in a pan with the butter and 1 garlic clove until golden. Pour the oil into a small bowl and add the rest of the garlic, chervil, and salt and pepper. Slowly whisk in the balsamic vinegar and set aside.

Boil the beans for 3½ minutes. Drain and refresh under cold water. Chop the beans in half. Place the tomatoes, potatoes, beans, and red onion into a salad bowl along with the lettuce, eggs, anchovy fillets and olives, drizzle over half the dressing, and then toss thoroughly. Serve with the tuna steak placed on top of the salad.

JP

MEAT

"Don't worry dear, I won't eat you." … But do we believe Jennifer?

CLARISSA WRITES: Since our last volume I am happy to report a number of vegetarians have been restored to the fold of meat-eaters. I have never understood the reasoning that if you don't like the way meat is reared or killed you turn vegetarian. Surely you should stand up and fight for changes and support the organic trade rather than risk your life with a paraquat-fed Third World carrot. Anyone who saw the quality of the Prince of Wales cattle herd when we filmed at Highgrove, and observed how happy and confident they were, would agree with me.

Jennifer has made the point that you can't really digest pork without its fat, but people forget this when buying meat. I spoke recently to a pig farmer who was telling me that the supermarkets are demanding leaner and leaner beasts, and as a result the pigs have no natural protection against the extremes of the weather and get sunburnt very easily. We filmed with a lot of very happy Gloucester Old Spot pigs in the Cotswolds, and it was great to see the boar and the sow lying about soaking up the sun, when they weren't trying to push Spike, our cameraman, off the bucket on which he was standing to film. Jennifer and I were taking bets on whether he would join them in the mud, but he managed to stay on his perch. The farmer said the young pigs needed a mud wallow to escape the danger of sunburn, which makes me worry for those so-called happy pigs

Happy Gloucester Old Spots out in the mud.

Clarissa hands out the rosettes at the pony club gymkhana.

standing around in shadeless fields.

What a wealth of variety we have lost with the unification of breeds of sheep. Recently I was preparing a lunch for the Duke of Hamilton and his Trustees at Lennoxlove House, where I am the in-house caterer, and complained to my butcher, Colin Peat of Haddington, that the chops he was offering were too large for what I required. "Well," he replied, "we'll just have to take them from a black-face sheep, they'll be smaller!"

Mutton is a strong flavor and we live increasingly in a country where the only acceptable strong flavor is a vindaloo curry. Curiously the only people in Britain who really still eat mutton are the Asian community. I was interested to see on the menu in a Birmingham balti house both curried lamb and curried mutton; elsewhere we have lost such distinctions of palate. What a bland and tasteless world we are heading toward so terrifyingly fast.

Our views on beef are well-known, and I don't want to bore you with reiteration, so I shall merely make the point that British beef is now the safest in the world. For one of the programs in the last series we cooked a splendid wing rib of beef from the Duke of Buccleugh's excellent outlet for the Gurkhas (as the men are Hindus and don't eat beef it wasn't our most tactful choice, but the officers were mostly British so it was okay). What a shame that when we went to Smithfield, London's meat market, this year we couldn't buy the same cut on the bone.

Pot Roast of Beef

This is a welcome winter dish which fills the house with delicious aromas. Try to get a well-hung joint of beef—it goes without saying, so I'll say it, the better the meat the better the pot roast.

2 pounds rump roast or bottom round
salt and freshly ground pepper

FOR THE MARINADE:
1 large onion, sliced
2 carrots, peeled and sliced
1 small turnip, chopped
2 cloves
1 bouquet garni
1 garlic clove, crushed
8 black peppercorns
2 tablespoons olive oil
2 tablespoons wine vinegar
2½ cups white wine

6 ounces pork fat, cut into lardons
4 cups beef stock
4 carrots, peeled and sliced
16 pearl onions
4 ounces mushrooms, sliced
2 tomatoes, peeled, seeded, and quartered
1 teaspoon sugar

Rub the meat with salt and pepper and place in a non-metallic bowl. Combine the ingredients for the marinade, pour over the meat, and refrigerate for 12–24 hours, turning the meat occasionally. Remove the meat from the marinade and dry thoroughly with paper towels. Strain the vegetables from the marinade and reserve both.

Fry the lardons in a skillet. Add the marinated vegetables, and cook until lightly golden. Remove the vegetables with a slotted spoon and put in the bottom of a flameproof casserole. Brown the meat in the hot pork fat on all sides and place on top of the vegetables. Pour a little of the fat out of the skillet and reserve. Add the marinade to the skillet, boil briskly, and stir. Transfer to a saucepan, scraping out any bits with a wooden spoon. Add the beef stock, bring to a boil, and boil briskly for a few minutes. Pour the stock over the beef in the casserole, and add more stock if it does not come halfway up the side of the beef. Bake in a preheated 300°F oven for 2½ hours.

Meanwhile, sauté the carrots gently in the reserved pork fat. Remove when cooked, then sauté the onions and mushrooms. Finally add the tomatoes and sugar, and set aside.

Remove the beef from the casserole and set aside. Mash the casseroled vegetables and strain this stock through a fine strainer, discarding the mashed vegetables. Allow the stock to cool a little and skim off as much of the excess fat as possible. Return the beef to the casserole, surround it with the sautéed vegetables, add the stock, replace in the oven, and cook for 1 hour. Remove the beef from the casserole to a serving platter, and arrange the vegetables around it. If the stock is not the correct consistency, reduce it further by boiling rapidly.

JP

Beef Stew with Prunes and Pumpkin Scones

Save British beef by eating more of it is what I say. This is a lovely rich, comforting stew for the cold winter months. The pumpkin scones can be served with the stew or put on top as a cobbler.

2 pounds stewing beef, cubed

FOR THE MARINADE:
1 bottle red wine
4 tablespoon olive oil
1 carrot, peeled and sliced
1 onion, sliced
2 garlic cloves, crushed
piece of orange peel
1 teaspoon juniper berries, crushed
pinch of grated nutmeg
2 sprigs of thyme
2 bay leaves, crushed
6 black peppercorns, crushed
2 tablespoons brandy (optional)

2 tablespoons beef dripping
1 pound prunes, soaked in water

FOR THE PUMPKIN SCONES:
½ cup (1 stick) butter, softened
¼ teaspoon ground nutmeg
salt and freshly ground pepper
½ cup cooked, mashed pumpkin
1 egg
½ cup milk
5⅓ cups all-purpose flour
1 teaspoon baking powder
milk, to glaze

1¼ cups beef stock
1 tablespoon all-purpose flour

Place the meat in a large non-metallic bowl. Combine all the ingredients for the marinade, pour over the meat, and refrigerate for 48 hours, turning the beef occasionally. Strain, reserving the marinade, and wipe the beef dry.

Brown the meat in the hot dripping. Transfer to a flameproof casserole and pour the marinade over. Cover and cook in a preheated 300°F oven for 2½ hours.

Meanwhile, drain the soaked prunes and simmer in a little salted water for 20–30 minutes, or until soft. When the meat has finished cooking, remove from the oven and set aside. Heat the oven to 425°F for the scones.

To make the scones, combine the butter, nutmeg, 1 teaspoon of salt, pepper to taste, and pumpkin in a bowl. Stir in the egg and add the milk. Sift in the flour and baking powder and mix to a soft dough. Turn onto a floured board and knead lightly. Roll out to ¾ inch thick and cut into circles using a small cup or biscuit cutter. Place on a greased baking sheet ½ inch apart and glaze with milk. Bake in the preheated oven for 15–20 minutes. Leave to cool slightly before serving with the stew.

To serve, remove the meat from the casserole and set aside. Reduce the meat juices by boiling rapidly. Stir the flour into the stock to make a paste and blend into the cooking juices. Push through a strainer with the vegetables. Return the meat and the prunes to the sauce and simmer gently on the stovetop for a further 15 minutes.

CDW

Beef in Pastry

This dish is also known as Beef Wellington, and I like to think it was created for the Duke of Wellington after his success at Waterloo. This recipe seems very complicated, I know, but well worth it and you can always buy refrigerated ready-made pie crust instead of making it. The pastry is prepared in two parts: a pie crust bottom to hold the beef, which avoids the sogginess imparted to flaky pastry by juices from the meat and mushrooms, and a flaky pastry top.

FOR THE MARINADE:
4 tablespoons light olive oil
2 medium carrots, peeled and sliced
2 medium onions, sliced
2 celery stalks, fibers removed and sliced
pinch of thyme and sage
1 bay leaf
4 cloves
6 black peppercorns

1 beef tenderloin, trimmed and tied, about 12 inches long
1 teaspoon salt
1 cup dry white vermouth
4 tablespoons brandy

FOR THE PASTRY DOUGH:
3 cups all-purpose flour
¾ cup plus 2 tablespoons (1¾ sticks) butter, chilled
4 tablespoons vegetable shortening
2 teaspoons salt
¾ cup water, chilled

vegetable oil

To prepare the marinade, heat the oil in a saucepan. Add all the vegetables, herbs, and spices, cover, and cook gently until tender. Place the beef in a long non-metallic dish or casserole, sprinkle with the salt, cover with the vegetable mixture, and pour the vermouth and brandy over. Cover and leave in a cool place or a refrigerator for 24 hours, turning and basting every few hours.

Meanwhile blend together the pastry ingredients. Chill for 2 hours before using. Butter the outside of a 12 x 3-inch bread pan. Roll out three-fifths of the pastry into a 16 x 7-inch rectangle, lay it over the upside-down pan, and press into place. Trim so the pastry forms a case of 1½ inches deep. Prick all over with a fork and chill for 30 minutes. Bake in the middle of a preheated 425°F oven until light brown, about 12–15 minutes. Cool for 10 minutes on the pan, then carefully unmold.

Scrape the marinade off the meat, reserve it for the sauce, and dry the meat with paper towels. Rub the meat with oil, place in a roasting pan, cover with oiled foil, and place in a preheated 425°F oven. Roast for 25 minutes, turning and basting halfway through the cooking time. Remove from the oven and leave to cool for 30 minutes.

Sauté the mushrooms and shallots in the butter for about 8 minutes. Add the Madeira, port, or sherry and boil rapidly until all the liquid evaporates. Stir in the pâté, mix well, turn into a bowl, and cover until needed.

Roll out the remaining pastry into a 16 x 7-inch rectangle. Spread

2 pounds mushrooms, finely chopped
5 shallots, finely sliced
4 tablespoons (½ stick) butter
½ cup Madeira, port, or medium-dry sherry
4 ounces (4 tablespoons) pâté de foie gras
6 tablespoons (¾ stick) butter, softened
1 egg, for glazing

FOR THE SAUCE:
2 teaspoons mushroom ketchup
2 cups beef stock
1 tablespoon tomato paste
1 tablespoon cornstarch
6 tablespoons Madeira, port, or sherry
salt and freshly ground pepper

half the softened butter over the bottom, and fold in half to enclose butter. Repeat with the remaining butter and fold again. Roll out into a rectangle, and fold in thirds, like a business letter. Chill for 2 hours. Remove from the refrigerator and roll out into another 16 x 10-inch rectangle to form a lid for the pastry case.

Place the baked bottom pastry case on a buttered baking sheet, and spread half the sautéed mushroom mixture on the bottom of the case. Remove the string from the beef, place it into the pastry case and cover with the rest of the mushrooms. Beat the egg with ½ teaspoon of water and paint the sides of the case. Place the pastry lid on top of the baked pastry case, press the edges together, and trim if necessary. Paint with the egg glaze. Cut crosshatch marks over the pastry and three vent holes 3 inches apart. Insert tiny foil funnels into these vent holes for escaping steam. Bake in the middle of a preheated 425°F oven for 20 minutes. Lower the heat to 375°F, and continue baking for a further 20 minutes before serving.

To make the sauce, simmer the marinade with the mushroom ketchup, beef stock, and tomato paste for 1 hour. When it has reduced to 2 cups, strain, return to the saucepan, and thicken with cornstarch mixed with the Madeira, port, or sherry. Simmer until shiny and thickened. Season to taste.

JP

Beef and Mushroom Croquettes with Sherry

Croquettes were commonplace when I was young as a way of using up the Sunday roast, cold with bubble and squeak for washday Monday and croquettes on Tuesday. They have fallen from fashion, but I still love them. This is a particularly tasty recipe and the sherry gives it a fine lift.

FOR THE WHITE SAUCE:
2 teaspoons all-purpose flour
2 teaspoons butter
⅔ cup milk

2 ounces mushrooms
¾ pound cooked beef
4 teaspoons butter
2 tablespoons sherry
parsley, finely chopped
salt and freshly ground pepper
all-purpose flour
dry bread crumbs
oil for deep fat frying

For the white sauce, first make a roux by melting the butter in a saucepan and stirring in the flour. Cook, stirring for 1 minute, until the mixture is cooked but not colored. Remove from the heat and gradually pour on the milk, whisking constantly. Simmer over gentle heat until the sauce has thickened.

Wash, trim, and chop the mushrooms. Finely chop the beef. Melt the butter in a skillet and sauté the mushrooms for 1 minute. Add the beef and sherry and season well. Cover and cook over a low heat for 5–10 minutes. Combine with the white sauce and parsley and allow to cool. The mixture should be well seasoned and very thick.

Chill the mixture and divide into croquettes the size of small potatoes. Roll in the flour and then in the bread crumbs. Fry in deep fat until golden brown. Serve with a tomato sauce or a mushroom and sherry sauce.

CDW

Carpetbag Steak

This is not really a carpetbag steak, it's a carpetbag roast. Redolent of an older age, maybe Dickensian, when huge steaks were eaten by gentlemen in their pubs and clubs. Curiously enough, the oysters impart a very good flavor to the beef, but do tell any guests in case they are allergic to the mollusk.

4-pound piece of boneless
lean beef, such as top loin
4 tablespoons (½ stick) butter
12–18 oysters, shucked
1½ cups sliced mushrooms
1½ cups fresh bread crumbs
grated zest of 1 lemon
1 tablespoon chopped parsley
salt and paprika, to taste
1 egg, beaten

Ask the butcher to make a pocket in the beef.

Melt the butter in a skillet. Add the oysters and mushrooms and cook for about 5 minutes. Transfer to a bowl, add the bread crumbs, lemon zest, parsley, seasonings, and beaten egg and stir together.

Stuff the mixture into the pocket of the beef and skewer, or sew the edges together. Roast in a preheated 325°F oven for 2 hours.

JP

Pickled Beef with Soda Scones

This is traditionally served at the Uphala festival in the Shetlands. I like to think of the Scots islanders carrying it as portable fare on their galleys and even the Norse Vikings before them. Once you have pickled your beef there are so many ways you can use it (see Boiled Beef with Lentils and Fennel, opposite).

Serves 8-10

3 pounds beef brisket
8 ounces coarse salt

FOR THE HERB AND SPICE MIX:
½ teaspoon ground allspice
½ teaspoon ground cloves
½ teaspoon ground nutmeg
pinch of thyme
black peppercorns, crushed
1 bay leaf, crushed
1 tablespoon saltpeter

¼ cup packed brown sugar
2½ tablespoons black treacle
or molasses
½ cup sliced carrots
½ cup finely chopped onion

FOR THE SODA SCONES:
3¼ cups all-purpose flour
2 teaspoons baking soda
2 teaspoons cream of tartar
1 teaspoon salt
6½ tablespoons lard or
vegetable shortening
1¼ cups buttermilk or soured
milk

Have the meat boned and trimmed, but not rolled. Rub well with the salt and leave overnight. Prepare the herb and spice mixture. Remove the beef from the salt and wipe dry. Rub the meat thoroughly with the herb and spice mixture and leave covered in a cool place for 2 days.

Add the sugar to the treacle and warm through until all the sugar crystals have dissolved. Pour over the meat, and spread carefully. Rub the spice and herb mixture into the meat every day for a week. The mix of herbs and spices will need to be replenished several time during this process.

At the end of the week, roll up the spiced beef and tie firmly with string. Put in a large pan of boiling water with the carrots and onion. Simmer gently for 3 hours. If serving cold, leave the meat to cool in the liquid.

To make the soda scones, sift the flour with the baking soda, cream of tartar, and salt. Rub in the lard to form a crumbly mixture, pour in the milk, and stir with a knife until the mixture is smooth. Shape into 2-inch circles about ½ inch thick. Place on greased baking sheets and bake in a preheated 425°F oven for 8-10 minutes until risen and golden.

CDW

Boiled Beef with Lentils and Fennel

A delicious way of using pickled beef. The fennel's aniseed flavor goes particularly well with the brisket and you can make the lentils as spicy as you wish.

3 tablespoons (⅜ stick) clarified butter
2 onions, chopped
1-inch piece of fresh gingerroot, finely chopped or
¼ teaspoon ground ginger
2⅓ cups brown lentils, soaked and drained
1 teaspoon turmeric
1 fresh chili, finely chopped
5 cups water
juice of ½ lemon
salt and freshly ground pepper
2–4 x 1-pound fennel bulbs
3 tablespoons olive oil
3 pounds pickled beef brisket (see page 80 for preparation)

Melt the clarified butter in a saucepan and fry the onions and the fresh or dried ginger. Add the lentils and stir in the turmeric and chili. Add the water and bring to a boil. Lower the heat and simmer covered for 15–20 minutes, adding more water if necessary, until the lentils are tender. Drain off any excess liquid, add a squeeze of lemon and season to taste.

Trim the fennel and cut each bulb in half. Put in a covered pan with the oil and more salt and pepper, cover tightly, and cook over medium heat for 10–15 minutes until tender, turning occasionally. Cut the fennel in half again and add to the lentils.

Slice the beef and serve on a bed of the lentils and fennel.

CDW

Lamb Kebabs with Spiced Eggplant Sauce

If you are a barbecue addict, this makes a change from charred raw sausages and salmonella. Just serve the aubergine sauce as a dip.

FOR THE MARINADE:
½ cup olive oil
juice of 1 lemon
1 garlic clove, finely chopped
1 large onion, finely chopped
1 teaspoon ground cumin
½ teaspoon ground coriander
½ teaspoon salt
½ teaspoon ground black pepper

2 pounds boneless lamb, cut into bite-size pieces
4 large tomatoes, cut into quarters
12 medium-size mushrooms, stems removed and halved
1 yellow bell pepper, seeded and cut into strips

FOR THE EGGPLANT SAUCE:
2 pounds eggplant
3 tablespoon olive oil
2 garlic cloves, chopped
1 teaspoon ground cumin
pinch of grated nutmeg
pinch of salt and freshly ground black pepper
juice of 1 lemon

1 tablespoon chopped parsley

Combine the marinade ingredients. Marinate the lamb, tomatoes, mushrooms, and yellow pepper for 2 hours, or overnight. Alternately thread the lamb, tomatoes, mushrooms, and yellow pepper onto soaked wooden or metal skewers.

To makes the sauce, slice the eggplants, place in a pie dish, pour the olive oil over, and sprinkle on the garlic, cumin, nutmeg, salt, pepper, and lemon juice. Cook in a preheated 400°F oven for about 30 minutes. Remove from the oven and leave to cool. Remove all the black skin, and squeeze the bitter juices out of the eggplants, and discard. Purée the flesh with the residue from the pie dish and pour into a saucepan.

Broil or grill the kebabs, turning them frequently. Heat the eggplant sauce, and stir in the chopped parsley. Serve the sauce with the cooked kebabs.

JP

Lamb in Phyllo Pastry

These dear little chops in their phyllo pastry could be described as a derivation from the ancient mutton pies, but are far more delicate. I would implore you to make sure they are nice and pink inside—do not overcook.

1 tablespoon vegetable oil
½ cup (1 stick) butter
1 medium onion, chopped
2 garlic cloves, crushed
½ pound mushrooms, sliced
1 tablespoon chopped parsley
1 tablespoon chopped mint
½ tablespoon chopped chives
pinch of thyme
juice of 1 lemon
salt and freshly ground pepper
½ cup fresh white bread crumbs
4 ½-pound lamb chops
12 sheets of phyllo pastry

Heat the oil with ¼ cup (½ stick) of the butter in a skillet. Add the chopped onion and garlic, and fry for a couple of minutes. Add the mushrooms and cook a little longer. Add the parsley, mint, chives, thyme, lemon juice, seasonings, and bread crumbs and fry until the crumbs begin to brown. Remove from the pan and set aside. Remove the bone from the chops, place into the skillet, and sear both sides.

Work with three 8 x 8-inch sheets of phyllo pastry at a time (if they are bigger there is too much overlap), and cover the rest with a damp cloth to prevent them drying out. Melt the remaining butter. Brush each sheet with melted butter before covering with the next sheet. When you have buttered three sheets, place a lamb chop in the middle, add a quarter of the mushroom stuffing, and fold the phyllo pastry over to make a parcel. Repeat with the remaining lamb chops and phyllo pastry. (When you are making the parcels make sure the ones you have done remain covered with a damp cloth.)

Put the parcels on a baking sheet and cook them in a preheated 400°F oven for 10 minutes. Reduce the heat to 350°F and cook for a further 30 minutes.

JP

Artichoke-Stuffed Lamb with Honey Tomato Sauce

There is an ancient Roman flavor about this method of serving lamb. The artichokes go very well with it, and while I know the tomatoes are post-Columbian, the honey, vinegar, and the onions keep the Epicurean theme.

10 raw artichoke bottoms, chopped
1 onion, chopped
1 tablespoon thyme
4-pound boned leg of lamb

FOR THE SAUCE:
8 tomatoes, skinned, seeded, and chopped
1 onion, finely chopped
2 tablespoons honey
2 tablespoons olive oil
1 tablespoon red wine vinegar
salt and freshly ground pepper

Mix together the artichokes, onion, and thyme. Spread out the piece of lamb, put the mixture on it, roll up the meat, and tie it securely. Roast in a preheated 350°F oven for 1½ hours, or until cooked through.

Meanwhile, simmer the tomatoes and onion with the honey, olive oil, and vinegar for 15 minutes. Purée the mixture, season, and add the skimmed cooking juices from the lamb. Serve with the meat.

CDW

Harrira

This Middle Eastern, somewhat peasant, stew is a useful and comforting supper dish, which is also good for using up the leftovers from a leg of lamb instead of buying fresh meat, should you so desire. Waste not, want not.

⅔ cup dried chick-peas (garbanzo beans)
1 large onion, chopped
1 tablespoon olive oil
2 tablespoons (¼ stick) butter
12 ounces boneless lamb, cubed into bite-size pieces
1 teaspoon ground ginger
1 teaspoon ground coriander
1 teaspoon turmeric
¼ teaspoon cayenne pepper
¼ teaspoon ground cinnamon
salt and freshly ground pepper
4–5 cups chicken stock
14 ounces chopped, or canned, tomatoes
heaping ¼ cup long-grain rice
pinch of saffron
1 red bell pepper, skinned, seeded, and cut into strips
juice of 1 lemon
1 tablespoon chopped parsley

Soak the chick-peas in water to cover by several inches overnight. Drain, rinse, and cook rapidly for 10 minutes. Lower the heat and simmer for a further 20 minutes. Drain.

Fry the onion in a skillet with the oil and butter until translucent. Add the cubed lamb and brown evenly. Add the ginger, coriander, turmeric, cayenne pepper, cinnamon, and salt and pepper to taste, and fry for a few minutes, stirring.

Transfer to a large saucepan or flameproof casserole. Add the chicken stock, cover, and cook gently for 1 hour. Add the chick-peas, tomatoes, rice, saffron, bell pepper, lemon juice, and leftover lanb if using, and cook for a further 30 minutes. Sprinkle with chopped parsley before serving.

JP

Kelp-Wrapped Lamb with Pickled Herring

This is an old Northumbrian dish which always amazes people when they discover what the stuffing is. You won't believe me until you try it, but it is delicious, so please do. The kelp is, quite frankly, a bit of a whim and the dish is just as good without it!

1 leg of lamb, main bone removed
salt and freshly ground pepper
6 sprigs of thyme
1 onion
6 rollmops (pickled Bismarck herring in spiced vinegar)
2 tablespoons fresh bread crumbs
large frond of kelp (use aluminum foil if not available)

Pierce the outer skin of the lamb, rub well with salt and pepper, and insert the sprigs of thyme. Chop together the onion and herrings, and mix with the bread crumbs, then season well. Stuff into the cavity in the lamb.

Wrap the lamb well in the kelp or the foil. Roast the lamb in a preheated 350°F oven for 20 minutes per pound.

CDW

Leg of Lamb with Chicken Liver Stuffing

A curious combination you may think, but fear not, a delight awaits all fearless culinary Trojans who are willing to embrace this slightly different receipt. The flavors are divine and the palate will be well rewarded.

4-pound boned leg of lamb
4 tablespoons (½ stick) butter
4 ounces chicken livers
1 medium onion, finely chopped
2 garlic cloves, crushed
2 tablespoons finely chopped celery
1 tablespoon chopped parsley
1 tablespoon chopped chives
⅓ cup cooked rice
salt and freshly ground pepper

Ask the butcher to remove the lamb bone, making sure he leaves a cavity for the stuffing.

Melt the butter in a skillet and fry the livers, lightly searing them. Chop the livers fairly small, then set aside. In the same pan, fry the onion, garlic, and celery until the onion is translucent. Add to the livers, with the parsley, chives, cooked rice, and salt and black pepper and mix together.

Put the stuffing in the cavity of the leg, cover the opening with aluminum foil, skewer or sew the other end with string, and place the meat in a roasting pan, foil side down. Roast in a preheated 350°F oven for 1 hour and 20 minutes, basting the meat occasionally.

JP

Lamb Casserole with Mint and Chick-peas

I can't remember where I found this Afghani recipe, designed for breast of lamb, but it has a good flavor. My friend Christine said she knew I could really cook when I used up the breasts of lamb in her freezer. I like the cut but it is fiddly, so you can use leg instead.

1⅓ cups dried chick-peas
(garbanzo beans)
½ cup olive oil
2 pounds boned leg or breast
of lamb, cut into pieces
2 onions, finely sliced
2½ cups water
handful of mint leaves,
chopped
½ teaspoon paprika
½ teaspoon turmeric
salt and freshly ground pepper
1 pound potatoes, peeled and
cut into large pieces
juice of ½ lemon

TO SERVE:
yogurt
finely chopped onion

Soak the chick-peas in water to cover by several inches for 12 hours. Drain and rinse. Drain again. Heat the oil in a large saucepan or flameproof casserole and brown the pieces of lamb. Add the onions and soften but do not allow to color. Add the chick-peas and water, bring to a boil, and skim well. Stir in the mint, paprika, turmeric, and salt and pepper. Lower the heat, cover, and simmer for 1 hour.

Add the potatoes, lemon juice, and more water if necessary, and continue cooking for 30 minutes, or until the potatoes and chick-peas are tender. Serve with yogurt to which you have added some finely chopped onion.

CDW

Ham with Pea Sauce

I love the combination of ham and peas. Be very careful when cooking your ham to ensure that the bubbles do not break the surface while it is simmering or the meat will be tough. My late brother and I spent many happy and inebriated hours watching our ham. I only hope someone cooks the ham for my funeral as painstakingly and lovingly as I did for his.

2–3-pound piece of ham or gammon, with rind removed
2½ cups vegetable stock
1¼ cups white wine
2 potatoes, peeled and cubed
1 carrot, peeled and cubed
1 parsnip, peeled and cubed
1 onion, finely chopped
⅔ cup sour cream
3 cups fresh shelled or frozen peas
salt and freshly ground pepper
1 tablespoon (⅛ stick) butter

Simmer the ham in the stock and white wine for 40–60 minutes (allowing 20 minutes per pound); top up with water if the ham is not completely covered. Remove from the stock and keep warm. Cook the potatoes, carrot, parsnip, and onion in the stock for about 5 minutes. Using a slotted spoon, remove the vegetables from the pan and set aside.

Boil the stock fiercely to reduce to about ¾ cup. Add the sour cream and peas and gently heat through without boiling. Purée in a blender, or push through a strainer, and season. Reheat the sauce gently, but do not let it come to a boil.

Sauté the drained root vegetables in a little butter until tender. Slice the meat thinly and serve with vegetables and sauce.

CDW

Pork Tenderloin with Celery Stuffing

I adore juniper berries and they certainly add zing to this delicious recipe for porky-worky.

2 pork tenderloins
½ cup (1 stick) butter
1 medium onion, finely chopped
2 garlic cloves, finely chopped
1 cup chopped celery
2 cups fresh white bread crumbs
2 tablespoons chopped parsley
½ teaspoon chopped fresh sage
¼ teaspoon chopped fresh rosemary
6 juniper berries, crushed
1 egg, lightly beaten
salt and freshly ground pepper
1 tablespoon olive oil
1¼ cups chicken stock
⅔ cup white wine
1 teaspoon grated lemon zest
beurre manié (see page 118)

Remove any fat and sinew from the tenderloins. Cut three-quarters through lengthwise, open out, cover with plastic wrap or waxed paper and flatten the tenderloins to about ¼ inch thick.

Melt 4 tablespoons (½ stick) of the butter in a saucepan. Add the onion, garlic, and celery and cook gently until softened but not brown. Add the bread crumbs, parsley, sage, rosemary, and juniper berries. Bind with the egg and season with salt and pepper. Spread the stuffing on the two flattened tenderloins, roll them up, and tie securely with string.

Melt a further 2 tablespoons of the butter in a skillet with the olive oil and brown the tenderloins. Butter a casserole with the remaining butter. Add the tenderloins and cook in a preheated 400°F oven for 40 minutes. Set the tenderloins aside and keep warm.

Add the chicken stock, wine and grated lemon zest to the casserole. Transfer the liquid to a saucepan and bring to a boil. Thicken with the beurre manié. Slice the pork tenderloins diagonally and moisten with a little of the sauce. Transfer the remainder of the sauce to a gravy boat.

JP

Pork with Clams

A well-known dish children love—Pork with Clams! As cooked for the Cotswold Hunt Pony Club, who relished this Portuguese import.

4 garlic cloves
2 teaspoons salt
1½-pound piece of boneless pork loin
2 tablespoons hot chili sauce
4 tablespoons lard or vegetable shortening
2 pounds Manila or littleneck clams

Combine the garlic and salt, and crush into a paste. Brush the meat with the paste, then the chili sauce, cover and refrigerate for 24 hours.

Cut the meat into cubes. Wash the clams thoroughly in several changes of water. Fry the meat in the lard for 10 minutes, or until brown. Add the clams and cook over a high heat so they open quickly, discarding any that do not open. Serve at once.

CDW

Illustrated overleaf

Pork Chops Marinated in Yogurt and Dill

I bought the carcasses of a couple of two-year-old organically raised Tamworth pigs. They were the size of the sides of Highland beef they were hanging next to in my butcher's, and quite delicious. But it means I have collected a few pork recipes. This is a good and easy way of preparing chops.

2 tablespoons hot chili sauce
1 cup thick plain yogurt
3 tablespoons chopped fresh dill
4 pork chops
oil
salt
coarsely crushed black peppercorns

Mix the chili, yogurt, and dill together, spread over the pork chops, and place in a plastic bag. Leave to marinate for 3–24 hours in the refrigerator.

Remove the chops from the marinade and pat dry. Brush with oil, sprinkle with salt and the crushed peppercorns and cook either under a broiler or on a cast-iron griddle. I cook the marinade thoroughly and serve it with the chops.

CDW

Veal Scallops with Spinach Stuffing

This is a very pretty dish and the mixture of spinach, rice, and vegetables is a great help to this really rather tasteless meat. If you can't get veal or have strong feelings toward little calves, then a pork tenderloin or turkey breast make a very nice scallop.

1 medium onion, finely chopped
1 garlic clove, finely chopped
6 tablespoons (¾ stick) butter
1 tablespoon vegetable oil
3 cups sliced mushrooms
¾ cup cooked spinach (measured after cooking)
¾ cup cooked rice
¼ teaspoon dried oregano
1 tablespoon chopped parsley
½ tablespoon chopped chives
salt and freshly ground black pepper
4 thin veal scallops
1 cup chicken stock

Soften the onion and garlic in 2 tablespoons (¼ stick) of the butter and ½ tablespoon of the oil. Add the mushrooms and cook together for a few minutes, stirring often. Squeeze any excess water from the spinach, chop it, and add to the mushroom mixture, along with the rice, herbs, and seasonings. Mix well. Spread the scallops with stuffing, roll up, and tie with string or secure with small skewers.

Melt the remaining butter and oil in a large skillet. Add the veal rolls and brown on all sides. Put the rolls in a baking dish, add the chicken stock, and cook in a preheated 325°F oven for 45 minutes.

JP

Stockbridge Marinated Venison

My friend Isabel Rutherford goes off every year to Skye. She stalks and, in her gum boots, climbs mountains that would challenge Sir Edmund Hilary. She returns with a battered ten-year-old stag, which even hounds might disdain, and serves it up chargrilled and tender as best tenderloin. I have wrung out of her the secret, although she is frightfully airy about this magic trick which even Escoffier might envy.

large piece of venison (allow 6 ounces of meat per person)
zest of 1 orange, finely pared
juniper berries
ground allspice
a bottle of ordinary red Bordeaux wine
a bottle of olive oil
salt and freshly ground pepper
red-currant jelly

Take your venison and painstakingly cut away all the fat and sinew, or "knicker elastic" as Isabel calls it. Put the trimmings in a large pot with the orange peel, juniper berries and allspice, and water and simmer away to form a good stock. (If you have an Aga leave the stock in the cool oven for 2 days to form a lovely jelly.)

Cut the remaining meat into boneless pieces and marinate them in an ocean of wine for 24 hours. Remove them, reserving the wine, pat them dry, and cover with olive oil. Add the wine to the stockpot. Leave the venison in the olive oil for another 24 hours.

Remove the venison from the marinade. Season and cook on a very hot griddle for a couple of minutes on each side. Leave to rest in a warm place for a few minutes and serve with gravy made from your stockpot.

CDW

Venison Pie

This is a good, robust single-crust pie, very medieval and, indeed, along with the pastry trimmings it used to be decorated with hounds and deer. Venison is a curious meat, very lean and so very easy to dry out and, when wild, too gamy for a lot of palates. In certain areas of Britain (usually around the old royal hunting forests) noone will touch it, which is, no doubt, a genetic legacy of the horrendous Norman game laws.

Serves 6–8

2 pounds boneless venison, such as neck, breast, flank or shoulder
⅓ cup seasoned all-purpose flour
4 tablespoons (½ stick) butter
⅔ cup port
juice of ½ lemon
1¼ cups venison stock
freshly grated nutmeg
pinch of thyme
salt and freshly ground pepper
¾ cups (1½ sticks) butter
1¼ pounds refrigerated ready-made pie crust or puff pastry dough, thawed if frozen
1 egg, beaten

Cut the venison into small steaks and dust with seasoned flour. Melt 1 tablespoon of the butter in a skillet. Add the steaks and sear quickly. Put the meat into a 2-2½ quart English pie dish or deep baking dish. Add the port, lemon juice, and stock, and sprinkle with grated nutmeg, thyme, and salt and pepper. Lay the remaining butter on top (traditionally it would have been lamb suet).

Roll out the pastry dough on a lightly floured board. Cover the top of the dish with the dough and glaze with the beaten egg. Bake in a preheated 425°F oven for 15 minutes, then bake at 350°F for 1¾ hours.

CDW

Tripe and Onions

I know many people who are passionate about tripe, Clarissa included, but it is the one bit of variety meat I have never come to terms with, and I have tried it in every possible way. Tripe afficionados, for whom I have cooked this, assure me it is a fine recipe.

1 pound tripe
1 bouquet garni
2 medium onions, sliced
salt and freshly ground pepper
4 tablespoons (½ stick) butter
⅓ cup all-purpose flour
1¼ cups milk
1 tablespoon chopped parsley

Cut the tripe into strips about 2 x ½ inches. Tripe is usually partly cooked by the butcher but you will need to cook it again. Place it in a saucepan, add 1½ cups water and bring to a boil for about 1 minute. Discard the water, add the same amount of fresh water and the bouquet garni, and simmer for about 1½ hours. Check to see that it is very tender. Add the onions to the pan and simmer for a further 30 minutes. Season to taste.

Melt the butter in a pan, add the flour, and stir with a wooden spoon to prevent the flour browning. Add the milk gradually, stirring continuously. Strain the liquid from the tripe saucepan, discarding the bouquet garni, and add it to the thickened sauce. Sprinkle in the parsley.

Put the tripe and onions into a serving dish and pour the parsley sauce over it.

JP

Yemeni Stew

This unusual stew was sent to me by Joan Saunders and her twin sister, but originates from Marcelle Thomal, whose grandfather was an orthodox Russian rabbi and whose grandmother's cookbooks have been handed down to him. As Raymond Sokolov explains in *The Jewish American Cookbook*, it is not widely known that innards once played a major role in Jewish cooking: sweetbreads, lungs, and, in the Middle East, penis were all commonly served.

1 pound of penis, ram's or bull's
3 tablespoons oil
1 onion, chopped
2 garlic cloves, peeled and chopped
1 teaspoon coriander seeds, crushed
1 large tomato, chopped
1 teaspoon cumin seeds, crushed
1 teaspoon salt
freshly ground black pepper

Scald the penis, then drain and clean. Place it in a saucepan, cover with cold water, and bring to a boil. Remove any scum, then simmer for 10 minutes. Drain and slice.

Heat the oil in a large skillet. Add the onion, garlic, and coriander and fry until the onion is golden. Add the penis slices and fry on both sides for a few minutes. Stir in the remaining ingredients with a good grinding of pepper, add enough water to cover, and bring to a boil. Lower the heat, cover, and simmer for about 2 hours, or until tender. Add a little water from time to time if necessary to prevent burning.

JP

POULTRY AND GAME

*Aliens on motorbikes? No, Clarissa and Jennifer dressed up
for bee-keeping.*

CLARISSA WRITES: One of the great mysteries of life is why so many people refuse to eat beef because of the BSE scare, which at worst (if you believe it and if you eat cheap beef) promises a one in six million risk, and prefer to eat chicken, which carries a high risk of salmonella. "Oh," you may say "but I buy those free-range chicken the supermarkets offer." Although these may taste better, the problem lies with the modern breeds, the speed with which they are raised, and what they are fed on. Five weeks from egg to table is a terrifying thought, and the flesh is loose on the bones, allowing disease to proliferate. The reason free-range chickens taste better rests in what they are fed, although they do not have much time to acquire any real flavor. The answer is to buy organically produced chickens of old breeds: then and only then will you know what chicken should taste like. Such chickens, however, are more expensive and although they go a lot farther, they are hard to get hold of. The answer is to use your chicken as a base for other flavors. The recipe for Mochrum Pie, for example, has an unusual use of apple with chicken.

Other poultry is a different matter. Ducks and geese are not raised on such a large commercial

"I'm ready for my close up, Mr. de Mille."

Whatever poultry you buy, try to buy the best flavor. When buying game go to a speciality store or use a mail-order supplier, and remember a young bird's beak and feet are relatively soft and pliable, while horney old claws are a sign to casserole the creature or put it in a pie. Game needs to be hung: even if you don't like a very strong flavor you must allow it to hang a while or it will be tough and tasteless.

scale so they tend to be better reared and have more flavor. Turkey, of course, is a breed apart. Even the most organically reared Bronze has not got a lot of flavor and the commercial ones have none at all. I suspect we only eat turkey for reasons of ritual and religion, and certainly if I weren't a food writer I wouldn't touch it from one year's end to the next.

What I really like is the game in this chapter. I love all game, and thank heavens the British hunting laws, our legacy from William the Conqueror, ensure it is still seasonal. Rabbit is the odd one out; don't buy imported rabbit, it's inferior, and in any event we have far too many of our own. Mine is shot for me by my young friend Sam Scott, but if you don't have access to such a hero, a good butcher will supply you.

If you live in a shooting area or with someone who shoots you will know all about a glut of game. When I worked on a pheasant farm we were endlessly looking for new ways to cook the ruddy things, yet I still love pheasant even after all that overexposure.

Collecting the honey at Wandlebury Ring with Bob Lemon, the beekeeper.

Maria's Spanish Chicken Andalouse

Serve this fragrant dish with some good plain, boiled rice of the long-grain variety. This makes a very good summer dish with a fine mixed salad on the side, some crusty bread, and a strong red wine such as Rioja.

3–4 pound chicken, cut into 8 serving pieces
¼ cup olive oil
4 tablespoons (½ stick) butter
16 pearl onions, peeled
2 teaspoons sugar
3 cups sliced mushrooms
2 garlic cloves, crushed
1 bouquet garni
1½ pounds tomatoes, skinned, seeded, and chopped
1 tablespoon tomato paste
3 tablespoons chicken stock or water
1 teaspoons wine vinegar
2½ cups white wine
½ teaspoon oregano
salt and freshly ground pepper
12 ripe olives
10 basil leaves, shredded

Sauté the chicken pieces in the olive oil until nicely colored. Transfer them to a flameproof casserole. In a separate pan, melt the butter, lightly glaze the pearl onions and add the sugar. Put the mushrooms, onions, garlic and bouquet garni in the casserole.

Mix the tomatoes, tomato paste, chicken stock or water, vinegar, wine, and oregano together in a saucepan. Bring to a boil and simmer for 10 minutes, stirring occasionally. Pour the mixture over the chicken in the casserole and add seasonings to taste. Cook in a preheated 375°F oven for 50–60 minutes. Stir in the olives and sprinkle the shredded basil leaves over the chicken before serving.

JP

Chicken with Cockle Sauce

I was giving a cookery demonstration in Dumfries, a part of Scotland separated from Cumbria only by the Solway Firth. During the book signing afterward I started talking to a most interesting woman who told me that in her part of Britain they cooked chicken with cockles. I tracked down the recipe and can recommend it to you.

5 cups cockles, well washed
1 boiling fowl or large free-range hen
1 onion, roughly chopped
1 celery stalk, chopped
salt and freshly ground pepper
2 egg yolks
2 tablespoons heavy cream
1¼ cups dry white wine
pinch of ground mace
pinch of cayenne pepper

Open the cockles by simmering them in a little salted water, then remove from their shells, reserving the juice.

Truss the fowl and fill the body cavity with two-thirds of the cockles, the onion and the celery, and season well. Cook in a clay roaster or in an earthenware jar set in boiling water on the stove-top, for about 2 hours, or until tender. (If you have neither a roaster nor a jar handy, wrap the bird tightly in several layers of aluminum foil, put in a roasting pan half full of water, and cook in a pre-heated 350°F oven.)

Remove the fowl and thicken the gravy with the blended egg yolks and cream. Add the remaining cockles, their juice, the wine, mace, cayenne and salt and pepper to taste.

Carve the bird and pour the sauce over.

CDW

Wylde Green Chicken

Commonly known as Wild Green Chicken. This is a dish I invented when staying with Christine, my best friend from schooldays, who lives in Wylde Green Road in Birmingham. It is a dish designed to deal with the problem of tasteless chicken, and it proved so popular with my godchildren I had to write it down.

Serves 6

2 tablespoons crunchy peanut butter
2 garlic cloves, finely chopped
2 tablespoons olive oil
6 chicken breast halves
1 teaspoon dried mustard
1 teaspoon paprika
1 teaspoon each salt and freshly ground pepper
1 teaspoon hot chili sauce
1 tablespoon dark rum or wine vinegar
1¼ cups water

Mix together the peanut butter, garlic, and half the oil. Lay the chicken breasts in a dish, pour the mixture over them, turning and working into the flesh. Leave to stand for at least 30 minutes.

In a large skillet, heat the rest of the oil and stir in the mustard, paprika, and salt and pepper. Tip the chicken breasts with the marinade into the pan and sauté until they are colored. At this stage I usually cut them into pieces in the pan. Add the chili sauce, rum or vinegar, and water and cook over a low heat until the chicken is cooked through, usually about 10 minutes. Serve with new potatoes or rice and a green salad.

CDW

Chicken Simla

Shades of the British memsahibs reclining in Simla. If you prefer, use a good curry paste which you can buy either hot or medium according to your taste. Though not a true Indian recipe, this is surprisingly good and can be eaten either hot or cold.

6 tablespoons (¾ stick) butter

3-pound chicken, cut into 8 serving pieces

1 medium onion, chopped

1 celery stalk, chopped into 1-inch pieces

1 sprig of parsley

1 sprig of fresh thyme

1 bay leaf

salt and freshly ground pepper

1 garlic clove, crushed

2 teaspoons curry powder

pinch of saffron

FOR THE BECHAMEL SAUCE:

1¼ cups milk

1 slice onion

6 black peppercorns

1 blade mace

1 bay leaf

1 tablespoon butter

1 tablespoon all-purpose flour

salt and pepper

freshly grated nutmeg

½ cup coconut milk

½ cup light cream

juice of 1 lemon

Melt the butter and gently fry the chicken pieces and onion until the chicken is a pale golden color; do not allow to brown. Lay the celery, parsley, thyme, and bay leaf in a casserole. Place the chicken pieces on top and sprinkle the salt and pepper, crushed garlic, curry powder and cooked onions over. Cook in a preheated 350°F oven for 35–40 minutes until the chicken is cooked through but not brown. Transfer the chicken to another clean casserole and return it to the oven to cook for a further 20 minutes while you prepare the sauce.

Meanwhile, infuse the saffron in 2 tablespoons of water.

To make the béchamel sauce, pour the milk into a saucepan. Add the onion slice, peppercorns, mace, and bay leaf. Bring almost to the boil, remove from the heat, cover and leave to infuse for about 20 minutes. Strain. Make a roux with the butter, flour and infused milk as described on page 78 but do not allow to thicken. Season the roux lightly with salt and pepper, and nutmeg. Return to the heat and cook, stirring until the sauce is thickened and smooth. Simmer gently for 2 minutes.

Stir the béchamel sauce and coconut milk in to the cooking juices in the first casserole. Transfer to a saucepan. Bring the sauce to a boil, lower the heat, and simmer gently for about 20 minutes stirring frequently. Strain into another pan. Add the cream and reheat, adding a little more coconut milk if the consistency is not quite right. Strain the infused saffron water and add to the sauce with the lemon juice. Pour the sauce over the chicken and serve.

JP

Calcutta Chicken Croquettes

My maternal grandfather died young of the demon drink, leaving my grandmother with two young children. Fortunately she met my step-grandfather, an extremely wealthy Sephardic Jew from Calcutta. For years she refused to marry him because he was a Jew and she was a Catholic. They lived together in great luxury with sixty indoor servants in what is now the British Residency in Singapore. I was reminded of this excellent dish by Claudia Roden's brilliant *Book of Jewish Food*, and dug out my step-great grandmother's version.

1½ cups cold cooked basmati rice (cook and drain but don't rinse, to leave in the starch)
1 pound finely ground chicken
2 onions, finely chopped
2–3 inch piece of gingerroot, grated
1 teaspoon garam masala
½ teaspoon turmeric
1 bunch cilantro, finely chopped
1 bunch flat-leaf parsley, finely chopped
4 tablespoons chicken fat or vegetable oil for frying

In a large bowl, mix together all the ingredients, except the chicken fat or oil. If the rice is not sticky enough you can add an egg to bind. (This can be done in a food processor, but I feel the resulting mixture doesn't have enough texture.) Form the rice mixture into 2 inch croquettes. Fry in the hot chicken fat or oil until deep golden brown.

CDW

Oriental Chicken Pudding

This looks magnificent when presented steaming at the table—full of different flavors and good for lunch on a cold winter's day. You could use suet instead of butter in the pastry. Great for hungry boys.

2 pounds boneless and skinless chicken breasts, cut into chunks
2½ tablespoons all-purpose flour
salt and freshly ground pepper
olive oil

FOR THE PASTRY DOUGH:
1 cup plus 1 tablespoon self-rising flour
1 tablespoon paprika
1 teaspoon ground mace
2 cups fresh white bread crumbs
2 teaspoons chervil
3–4 pinches of cayenne pepper
salt
¾ cup (1½ sticks) butter, frozen
1 egg

3 heads Belgian endive
2 tablespoons freshly chopped cilantro
1 bunch scallions, chopped
2 large garlic cloves
coarsely grated zest and juice of 1 lemon
1 tablespoon soy sauce
2-inch piece of fresh gingerroot, grated

Coat the chicken pieces with the all-purpose flour seasoned with salt and pepper. Heat the olive oil in a heavy-bottomed pan over a high heat. Add the chicken pieces and brown on all sides, then set aside to cool.

To make the pastry dough, mix together the self-rising flour, spices, bread crumbs, chervil, cayenne pepper, and salt to taste in a bowl. Hold the butter at one end with a damp cloth and grate it into the bowl, mixing with your hands. Whisk the egg in a measuring cup and top up with water to a total of ¾ cup. Gradually stir the liquid into the flour and butter. Bring it together and form a ball. Save one-quarter of the dough for a lid. Roll out the rest of the dough thinly into a circle with a diameter of about 14 inches. Line a 7½ cup pudding bowl or deep baking bowl with the dough, leaving the edges to overlap the top of the bowl. Don't worry if the dough breaks, just gently patch it together with your hand.

Cut the Belgian endive into thick slices and mix with the cilantro, scallions, garlic, lemon zest, soy sauce, ginger, and chicken. Add the lemon juice and season. Spoon this mixture into the bowl so that it forms a mound at the top. Fold the dough over the filling and wet the edges. Roll out the reserved dough into a circle big enough to form a top. Seal the edges by pressing them lightly. Cover with a buttered piece of waxed paper and make a pleat in the middle before putting it over the top of the pudding. Put a piece of aluminum foil loosely over the paper and tie both securely with string. Make a handle with string and lower the pudding into a saucepan of boiling water. Cover and boil gently for 3 hours. Check the water level at regular intervals and top up as required.

JP

Chicken with Red Pepper Sauce

It is always useful to have different ways to prepare chicken, fast becoming the staple food in many a household. Do try to get a chicken which has run naked and unencumbered throughout its formative years—otherwise known as free range. It really does make all the difference, and the bones make wonderful stock.

4 tablespoons (½ stick) butter
2 tablespoons vegetable oil
6 small shallots, chopped
2 red bell peppers, seeded and chopped
2 garlic cloves, chopped
3 pound chicken, cut into 8 serving pieces
⅔ cup white wine
salt and freshly ground pepper
1 teaspoon dried oregano
1 tablespoon tomato paste
1 tablespoon chopped parsley

Melt the butter with the vegetable oil in a large skillet. Add the shallots, bell peppers, and garlic and fry gently until the shallots and pepper are just soft. Remove with a slotted spoon and set aside. Turn up the heat and fry the chicken pieces on both sides.

Put the chicken pieces in a casserole, spoon the peppers and shallots on top, pour in the wine, add 1 teaspoon of salt and ½ teaspoon of pepper and the oregano.

Cook in a preheated 375°F oven for 45–55 minutes. Remove the chicken pieces and pour the liquid with the peppers, shallots, and garlic into a blender or food processor. Add the parsley and purée. Pour the sauce over the chicken pieces and serve.

JP

Mochrum Chicken Pie

Flora Stuart, president of the Belted Galloway Society (Belted Galloways are famous beef cattle), served me this recipe, an invention of her butler John. She lives in a romantic fourteenth-century castle called Old Place of Mochrum, hence the name. When she served this pie to me I couldn't guess what the topping was just by looking at it, as it has an interesting pale green color. It is a great pie and just as good cold as hot.

4 cooking apples
3 onions, chopped
4 tablespoons (½ stick) butter
salt and freshly ground pepper
½ pound refrigerated ready-made pie crust
1 pound cooked chicken meat

Peel, core, and chop the apples. Place them in a saucepan with a little water and cook until they form a purée. Fry the onions in the butter until soft and colored, season, and leave to cool.

Cut the dough into two portions, one larger than the other. Roll the bigger portion to a large circle and line a deep pie dish or baking dish with the rolled-out dough. Place the onions in the bottom, then the chicken meat on top and level off. Heap the apple on top of the chicken, mound it slightly, and cover with a lattice of dough made from the remaining portion of dough. Bake in a preheated 425°F oven for 10 minutes. Lower the heat to 350°F and continue baking for a further 30 minutes.

CDW

Chicken, Polenta, and Quail Egg Pie

This is a very good pie to take cold on a picnic or even lukewarm if you have just baked it. The five-spice powder gives a hint of China, which is a change from Branston pickle.

4-pound chicken, cut into 8 serving pieces
2½ cups chicken stock
1¼ cups white wine
1 large onion, sliced
1 bay leaf
10 black peppercorns
1 heaped teaspoon five-spice powder
1½–2 tablespoons polenta or cornmeal
juice of 1 lemon
4 tablespoons (½ stick) butter
6 ounces bacon, cut into narrow strips (lardons) and cooked until crisp
8 hard-boiled quail eggs, peeled
salt and freshly ground pepper
½ pound refrigerated ready-made pie crust
beaten egg, to glaze

Put the chicken pieces in a saucepan and cover with the chicken stock and the wine. Add the onion, bay leaf, peppercorns, and five-spice powder. Bring to a boil, lower the heat, and simmer gently for 45 minutes. Remove from the heat and stir in the polenta or cornmeal, lemon juice, and butter. Simmer for another 15 minutes or so until you think the chicken is tender. Remove the saucepan from heat and set aside to allow the chicken and stock to cool.

Skin and bone the chicken pieces. Place the chicken meat in a large, deep pie dish or deep baking dish. Add the bacon, quail eggs, and the stock from the pan. Taste for seasoning. Roll out the dough on a lightly floured board and cover the pie dish with the dough. A nice glaze can be obtained by brushing the dough with a beaten egg. Bake in a preheated 400°F oven for 25–30 minutes, or until golden.

JP

Wild Duck with Sauce Bigarade

Bigarade is the French name for bitter Seville oranges which only have a short season, so grab them when you can during February. The sauce is most excellent with mallard or wild duck, enriching the rather dry flesh. Otherwise, serve the sauce with a domestic duck or pieces thereof. The ducks should be served pink inside which takes about 30 minutes in a preheated oven at 350°F. If you want to make this sauce when Seville oranges are out of season, cheat by using 1 ordinary orange and 1 heaping tablespoon of bitter marmalade, but omit the sugar.

2 4-pound ducks of your choice with giblets
1 onion, chopped
1 large carrot, peeled and chopped
1 bouquet garni
2½ cups water

FOR THE SAUCE:
2 Seville oranges
2 tablespoons (¼ stick) butter
1 level tablespoon all-purpose flour
1 cup chicken or game stock
2 teaspoons sugar
salt and freshly ground pepper
Madeira or port

Make a stock with the duck giblets, onion, carrot, and bouquet garni. Meanwhile, roast the ducks in a preheated 350°F oven for 20–30 minutes, depending on the degree or rareness you like.

To make the sauce, pare the peel off the oranges very thinly so no pith is left. Cut into tiny strips and fling into a pan of boiling water for 5 minutes to blanch. Drain well and set aside. Melt the butter in a little saucepan. Stir in the flour and cook gently until it becomes a pale coffee color. Add the stock a little at a time, skimming, until a smooth sauce forms and continue simmering for a further 15 minutes. Add the blanched peel and the sugar, season to taste, and add the juice from the roasting pan after you have drained off the fat.

JP

115

Wild Duck with Barley

There seems to be an attempt to make barley a fashion food item, although one attempt at eating a barley risotto cures most people. I, however, am very fond of barley properly utilized. Try this curious way of preparing it which comes from a Swedish recipe, and which I think goes well with the richness of the duck.

2 wild ducks, if possible with their livers, dressed
salt and freshly ground pepper
4 ounces prunes
3 apples, chopped
butter, softened
juice of 1 orange
2 tablespoons honey
1 tablespoon red wine vinegar
2 tablespoons vegetable oil
⅔ cup Scotch barley, cooked
¼ cup thick plain yogurt
2 tablespoons fresh grated horseradish
2 cups water

Rub the outside of the ducks with salt and pepper. Stuff with the prunes, apples, and livers. Smear with soft butter and roast in a preheated 450°F oven for 20–30 minutes depending on the rareness preferred, basting occasionally.

In a saucepan, boil together the orange juice, honey, vinegar, and oil for a few minutes. Stir in the barley and season. Add the yogurt and the horseradish and heat through.

When the ducks are cooked, make a thin gravy from the juices and the water. Carve the ducks and serve on the barley with the gravy on the side.

CDW

Duckling with Green Grapes

Green grapes are usually identified with recipes called Veronique, but not in this case. The sweetness of the grapes with the damson jelly goes very well with duckling and cuts the fatty content of the bird. A good dinner party dish when served with a purée of celery root and potato.

5-pound duckling
salt and freshly ground pepper
12 ounces white seedless grapes
2 tablespoons brandy
⅔ cup dry white wine
1 tablespoon damson jelly
1 bouquet garni
¼ teaspoon grated nutmeg
1 tablespoon chopped parsley
1 tablespoon cornstarch

Prick the duck all over and rub salt and pepper onto the skin. Put in a roasting pan in a pre-heated oven at 425°F for 30 minutes until the duck is light brown.

While the duck is roasting, wash and drain the grapes. Purée the grapes, reserving a few for decoration. Take the duck out of the oven and lower the heat to 350°F.

Heat the brandy in a ladle, ignite it and pour over the duck. Cut the duck into serving portions and put it into a flameproof casserole. Discard the fat from the roasting pan. Pour the puréed grapes, and wine into the roasting pan. Add the damson jelly, bouquet garni, nutmeg, and parsley. Stir with a wooden spoon, making sure you scrape up all the brown bits in the roasting pan. Pour the liquid over the duck portions in the casserole, cover, and cook for a further 45–60 minutes.

Remove the duck portions from the casserole, discard the bouquet garni, and thicken the liquid with the cornstarch dissolved in a little water. Add the remaining grapes. Pour some of the sauce over the duck and put the remainder in a gravy boat.

JP

Duck in Red Wine Sauce

This is a useful dish to prepare in advance if you are a working person. Just heat it up before you need to eat it. As with many a casserole dish, the flavors intensify on reheating.

4-pound duck, cut into serving pieces
salt and freshly ground pepper
2 tablespoons all-purpose flour
4 tablespoons (½ stick) butter
2 tablespoons olive oil
½ cup chopped shallots
4 ounces bacon, cut into narrow strips (lardons)
1¼ cups red wine
6 crushed black peppercorns
1 bay leaf
2½ cups chicken stock
16 whole pearl onions
1 teaspoon sugar
3 cups sliced mushrooms

FOR THE BEURRE MANIÉ:
3 tablespoons (⅜ stick) butter, softened
2½ tablespoons all-purpose flour

Sprinkle the duck pieces with salt, pepper, and flour. Melt 2 tablespoons of the butter and 1 tablespoon of oil in a large skillet and sauté the duck pieces until golden brown. Place the duck pieces in a casserole. Cook the shallots and bacon in the oil and butter in the skillet for a few minutes. Add the wine, peppercorns, and bay leaf. Bring to a boil to reduce by half, then add the stock and again reduce by half. Strain the sauce over the duck and cook gently in a preheated 375°F oven for 1 hour, but check to make sure the duck pieces are cooked.

Meanwhile, melt the remaining butter and oil in the skillet. Add the onions, sprinkle with sugar, and fry until brown. After the duck has been cooking for 30 minutes, add the onions and the mushrooms.

When the duck pieces are cooked, set them aside. Check the sauce for consistency and seasoning and, if necessary, thicken with the beurre manié. To make this, knead the butter and flour together and form into a small knob.

JP

Grouse Pie

If you have a good game dealer he may sell you old grouse quite cheaply as everyone wants the young birds for roasting. This is a flavorsome robust country pie and the gravy is enriched by the addition of steak. This was a custom which grew in the Georgian age with the greater availability of beef, thanks to the Agricultural Revolution.

Serves 4-6

brace of grouse, dressed
1 pound beefsteak, such as
rump or top round
½ cup diced slab bacon
2 hard boiled eggs, peeled
salt and freshly ground pepper
pinch of ground mace
pinch of ground nutmeg
2½ cups game stock
1 tablespoon sherry
1¼ pounds puff pastry dough
beaten egg, to glaze

Divide each grouse into four leg and four breast pieces. Cut the beef into 1-inch cubes. Place the meat in a large, deep pie dish or deep baking dish and top with the bacon and the hard-boiled eggs. Add salt and pepper to taste, the mace, and nutmeg. Pour in enough stock to cover. Put a lid on the dish, or cover with aluminum foil, and cook in a preheated 325°F oven for 1½ hours. Remove from oven and turn the heat up to 425°F.

Leave the dish to cool slightly. Add the sherry. Cover with a lid of the puff pastry, glaze with the beaten egg, and bake for a further 30 minutes. Serve with creamed potatoes and green vegetables.

CDW

Guinea Hen with Jerusalem Artichokes, Mushrooms, and Pearl Onions

For those who are a little faint of heart and do not like the strong flavor of a well-hung pheasant, this provides an ideal alternative. Guinea hens can be dry, but this recipe works a treat every time.

1 large plump guinea hen, or 2 small ones, dressed
1 tablespoon vegetable oil
½ cup (1 stick) butter
4 shallots, finely chopped
1 garlic clove, crushed
3 cups sliced mushrooms
1 pound Jerusalem artichokes, peeled
16 pearl onions
1 tablespoon sherry, warmed
⅔ cup light cream
2 egg yolks, beaten
salt and freshly ground pepper
1 tablespoon chopped parsley

Brown the guinea hen in the oil and half the butter in a large skillet. Transfer to a casserole. Fry the shallots and garlic and add to the casserole. Cook the guinea hen in a preheated 375°F oven for 1 hour.

Meanwhile, gently fry the mushrooms in the fat remaining in the skillet for 2–3 minutes. Cut the artichokes into fairly uniform pieces. Parboil the pearl onions and artichokes for no more than 5 minutes. Strain. Add the mushrooms, onions, and artichokes to the casserole and continue cooking for a further 30 minutes.

Remove the casserole from the oven, pour the heated sherry over the guinea hen and ignite. Remove the hen and cut into serving pieces. Arrange them on a serving dish with the vegetables around them and keep warm.

Stir the cream into the juices remaining in the casserole with a wooden spoon, pour the juices into a saucepan and boil rapidly to reduce. Remove from the heat and stir in the egg yolks with salt and pepper to taste. Pour a little sauce over the guinea fowl and sprinkle with the chopped parsley. Serve the remainder of the sauce in a gravy boat.

JP

Pheasant with Chestnuts in Pastry

When I worked on the pheasant farm in Sussex I learnt to sympathize with those who have endless pheasants to cook and spent a lot of time thinking up recipes. I particularly like this one because it is so good for a dinner party. You can get to the stage where you wrap the pheasant earlier in the day and just bung it in the oven at the relevant time, and the pastry stops the meat drying out. This is also a good recipe for guinea hens and chickens.

1 pound chestnuts
½ pound pheasant or chicken livers, chopped
½ pound slab bacon, ground
2 onions, chopped
6 tablespoons (¾ stick) butter
salt and freshly ground pepper
1 pheasant, dressed
1¼ cups game or chicken stock
1 pound puff pastry dough
1 egg yolk, beaten

FOR THE SHERRY SAUCE:
6 tablespoons (¾ stick) butter
scant ⅓ cup all-purpose flour
3 cups chicken stock
salt and pepper
3 tablespoons heavy cream
3 tablespoons dry sherry

Peel the chestnuts and simmer in salted water until tender but still whole. Mix together the chestnuts, livers, bacon, onion, 2 tablespoons of the butter, and salt and pepper to taste. Stuff the pheasant with the mixture. Brown the pheasant in the rest of the butter in a flameproof casserole. Add the stock and roast in a preheated 400°F oven for 20 minutes, turning onto the other side half way through and basting frequently. Remove from the oven and leave to cool.

Roll out the pastry dough on a lightly floured surface and wrap the bird in it. Cut a slit for steam and brush with the egg yolk. Bake at 375°F for 40 minutes.

Meanwhile, to make the sauce, melt 4 tablespoons (½ stick) of the butter in a heavy-bottomed pan. Add the flour and cook for 3 minutes, stirring continuously, to make a roux. Add the stock to the roux a little at a time. Whisking continuously, reduce the heat and simmer for 30 minutes, stirring and skimming every 10 minutes. Add the cream and simmer over a low heat for 10 minutes. Season and pass through a conical strainer into a clean saucepan. Over a low heat, whisk in the remaining butter a little at a time. Remove from the heat and add the sherry. Serve with the pheasant.

CDW

Pheasant with Cranberries, Red Wine, and Port

I really prefer a traditionally cooked pheasant with all the trimmings. However, if you belong to a sporting family and have a plethora of the birds this makes a welcome change.

4 tablespoons (½ stick) butter
2 young pheasants, dressed
1 onion, halved
1 cup chicken stock
1 cup red wine
¼ cup port
2 tablespoons French mustard
juice of 1 orange
juice of 1 lemon
4 tablespoons cranberry sauce
salt and freshly ground pepper

FOR THE BEURRE MANIÉ:
3 tablespoons butter, softened
2½ tablespoons all-purpose flour

Spread 2 tablespoons of the butter over each bird and put half an onion in each cavity. Roast the pheasants breast-side up in a preheated 350°F oven for about 1 hour. After 30 minutes, baste and turn the pheasants breast-side down.

Meanwhile, place the chicken stock, red wine, port, mustard, orange and lemon juices, and cranberry sauce in a saucepan. Bring to a boil and simmer for 20 minutes. To make the beurre manié, knead the butter and flour together and form into a small knob.

Remove the pheasants from the casserole and set aside. Stir the juices left in the casserole into the saucepan and while it is simmering thicken it with knobs of the beurre manie.

JP

123

Pheasant with Lemon and Capers

I first made this dish at a Red Cross demonstration in Dumfries for Eileen Duncombe. I was somewhat alarmed when I discovered the organizers were going to raffle the food as this was an untried dish. So busy am I these days that I have to invent recipes every time I'm near a stove. However, I'm happy to say this was a success—new pheasant recipes are always welcome.

1 pheasant, dressed and cut into pieces
finely grated zest and juice of 4 lemons
¾ cup plus 1 tablespoon all-purpose flour
salt and freshly ground pepper
¼ cup vegetable oil
1 tablespoon drained capers, roughly chopped
½ cup brown sugar
1¼ cups game or chicken stock

Marinate the pheasant pieces overnight in the lemon juice.

Remove the meat from the marinade, reserving the juice, and pat dry with paper towels. Coat the meat with seasoned flour. Brown the strips in the oil in a heavy-bottomed pan. Add the capers, lemon zest and brown sugar and cook for 2–3 minutes. Heat the stock and lemon juice together and serve as a sauce.

CDW

Cream-Smothered Pheasant

For people with an endless supply of the little creatures, another way to enjoy pheasant.

1 large or 2 small pheasants, dressed
1 tablespoon vegetable oil
6 tablespoons (¾ stick) butter
1 medium onion
2 garlic cloves
2 cups white wine
1 cup stock, made from giblets minus the liver
1 bouquet garni of parsley, bay leaf, and thyme
pinch of grated nutmeg
salt and freshly ground pepper
2 tablespoons all-purpose flour
1 cup heavy cream
3 egg yolks, beaten
1 tablespoon chopped parsley

Sauté the pheasant in the oil and 4 tablespoons of the butter in a skillet until golden brown all over. Put the pheasant in a casserole. Fry the onion and garlic in the skillet, but do not brown. Add the wine, stock, bouquet garni, nutmeg, and salt and pepper and bring to a boil. Pour over the pheasant. Cook in a preheated 400°F oven until the pheasant is tender, about 1–1½ hours. Transfer the pheasant to the serving dish and keep warm. Boil the casserole juices in a saucepan to reduce by half.

Melt the remaining butter in a saucepan. Add the flour, stir and cook for a few minutes. Gradually add the pan juices, stirring constantly, then stir in the cream. Lower the heat and simmer for a few minutes. Remove the saucepan from the heat and stir in the beaten egg yolks. Test for seasoning and sprinkle with parsley. Pour a little over the pheasant and serve the remainder in a gravy boat.

JP

Rabbit Isabel

My friend Isabel produced this recipe for me from the Scottish Borders. I cooked it at the Scone Palace Game Fair, which is a great event of the Scottish year, originally set up by my friend Henry Crichton-Stuart. When I demonstrated this recipe I was presented with two whole rabbits, which I cut up on stage. This is a fine recipe for using all the rabbit, and is delicious and economical.

2½ tablespoons all-purpose flour
salt and freshly ground pepper
¼ teaspoon dry mustard
¼ teaspoon cayenne pepper
4 young rabbits, tenderloins and leg meat removed
1 egg white
4 slices good bacon
sorrel or sage leaves
½ cup (1 stick) butter
1 onion, finely chopped
½ cup white wine

Season the flour with salt and pepper, dry mustard, and cayenne pepper, and set aside.

In a food processor, finely grind the rabbit leg meat, add the egg white and seasoning, and blend to a paste. Flatten the tenderloins and flour lightly. Cut the slices of bacon in half, each to fit on one tenderloin. Lay a piece of bacon onto four of the tenderloins, spread a layer of the mousseline of rabbit and egg white onto the bacon, and lay your sorrel or sage leaves on top of this. Place the other rabbit tenderloins on top of each to make a package.

In a heavy-bottomed skillet with a cover, melt the butter. Add the onion and gently fry. Add the rabbit packages, one by one, and brown, turning carefully. Season, pour in the white wine, cover, and cook gently for 10 minutes, turning the packages over halfway through. Check that the rabbit is tender, and serve with garlic-flavored mashed potatoes and a green vegetable.

CDW

Illustrated on previous page

Rabbit with Chocolate

This is a very early Spanish recipe which was presumably brought back from the New World. As they have no rabbits in Mexico or South America, I imagine the dish was designed for guinea pig or even chihuahua. However, it works very well with rabbit and has an excellent flavor.

4 tablespoons lard
4 ounces salt pork, finely diced
2½ tablespoons all-purpose flour
salt and freshly ground pepper
2–3-pound rabbit, cut into 8 serving pieces
12 shallots, peeled
¼ cup dry red wine
½ cup water
1 bay leaf
handful of chopped parsley
generous pinch of thyme
6½ tablespoons blanched almonds
¼ cup pine nuts
1½ teaspoons finely grated bittersweet chocolate

In a flameproof casserole, melt the lard and fry the pork until crisp and browned. Transfer to paper towels to drain. Mix together the flour and salt and pepper and coat the rabbit pieces. Brown them carefully in the fat in the pan and transfer to a plate. Fry the shallots in the fat and add to the plate with the rabbit. Deglaze the casserole with the wine and water, return the pork and rabbit, and add the bay leaf and herbs. Reduce the heat to low, cover, and cook gently for 30 minutes.

Grind the almonds and pine nuts in a blender or with a mortar and pestle, and combine with the grated chocolate. Add this and the onions to the rabbit, stir thoroughly, and add a little more wine if dry. Cover again and continue cooking for a further 30 minutes, or until rabbit is tender. Serve at once.

CDW

Baked Rabbit

I know some people won't eat rabbit for various reasons, but I wish they would try. The flesh is succulent with a good flavor—it has little or no fat and can only be commended in every way. The wilder the rabbit the better the flavor, and you will be doing the farmers a great favor.

FOR THE MARINADE:
1 cup red wine
1 cup red wine vinegar
1 garlic clove, chopped
2 celery stalks, chopped
sprig of thyme
sprig of parsley

1 rabbit, cut into serving
pieces
2½ tablespoons all-purpose
flour
2 tablespoons olive oil
2 slices slab bacon, diced
1 large onion, thickly sliced
1 large garlic clove, finely
chopped
½ teaspoon paprika
1¼ cups dry white wine
1 tablespoon tomato paste
1 bay leaf
salt and freshly ground pepper

Mix together all the ingredients for the marinade. Place the rabbit pieces in the marinade and refrigerate overnight, preferably, or for at least several hours.

Remove the rabbit pieces from the marinade, dry with paper towels, and dust lightly with flour. Heat the olive oil in a skillet. Add the rabbit pieces and fry until light golden brown. Transfer to a casserole.

Sauté the bacon and onion in the skillet. Add the garlic and paprika and cook a little longer. Add the wine, tomato paste, bay leaf, and salt and pepper. Bring to a boil, lower the heat, and simmer for about 5 minutes. Pour over the rabbit and cook in a preheated 350°F oven for about 1½ hours, or until the rabbit is tender.

CDW

Burnett's Woodcock

My friends Jane and George, to whom this dish is dedicated, are known as the Dona-kebabs because they gave me a sheep for my fiftieth birthday and called it Kebab to guard against sentimentality. George is a keen shot and is always looking for different ways of preparing woodcock. You can use wood pigeon if you are not so fortunate.

FOR THE POTATO CAKES:
1½ pounds waxy potatoes, peeled
2 egg whites and 1 egg yolk
1 tablespoon drained capers, chopped
⅔ cup whipping cream
2 tablespoons (¼ stick) butter

4 woodcock, properly hung
½ cup (1 stick) butter, softened
4 slices bacon

FOR THE SAUCE:
4 pigeon livers (use pheasant or chicken livers if not available)
4 tablespoons (½ stick) butter
½ cup white wine
2 tablespoons beef stock
10 juniper berries, crushed
squeeze of lemon juice
salt and freshly ground pepper

First make the potato cakes. Boil the potatoes, mash them, and let them dry well. Beat the egg whites until very stiff, but not dry. Stir the egg yolk, capers, and cream into the mash and fold in the egg whites. Form small cakes and fry in the butter until brown.

Spread each woodcock generously with butter and cover with a slice of bacon. Roast in a preheated 425°F oven for 10–15 minutes, depending on how you like them, more if you must.

For the sauce, sauté the livers in butter until just cooked. Mash and push the livers through a fine strainer. Put the liver purée in a pan and thin with white wine and stock. Add the juniper berries, lemon juice, and salt and pepper. Simmer for a few minutes.

Place the roasted woodcock on the potato cakes and serve with the sauce.

CDW

Turkey Pilaf in Phyllo Pastry

I am not a great fan of turkey, but I am always being asked for ways of using it and there is no doubt that if you cook one there will be leftovers. A pilaf is an interesting Persian dish, and enclosed in phyllo pastry this has a Turkish flavor, even if the name of the bird is merely a historical mistake.

¾ cup (1½ sticks) butter
1 onion, finely chopped
⅓ cup pine nuts
1 heaping cup long-grain rice
2½ cups chicken stock
2 tomatoes
2 tablespoons currants
½ teaspoon ground allspice
pinch of grated nutmeg
½ teaspoon sugar
½ teaspoon cayenne pepper
salt and freshly ground pepper
½ red bell pepper, chopped
1 celery stalk, chopped
1 small zucchini, chopped
4 chicken livers, chopped
½ pound raw or cooked turkey, sliced in thin strips
grated zest and juice of 1 lemon
8 sheets phyllo dough
melted butter

In a large pan, melt ½ cup (1 stick) of the butter. Add the onion and fry until soft. Add the pine nuts and rice and cook over medium heat until lightly colored. Add half the chicken stock, a little at a time to allow the rice to absorb it. Stir in the tomatoes, currants, spices, sugar, cayenne pepper, and salt and pepper. Pour in the rest of the chicken stock and bring to a boil. Lower the heat, cover, and simmer until the rice is tender and the stock is absorbed, about 15–20 minutes.

In a small pan, melt the remaining ¼ cup of butter. Add the bell pepper, celery, and zucchini and sauté. Add the chicken livers and turkey strips, if uncooked, season, and cook until the chicken livers are just done. Add this to the rice mixture with the lemon zest and juice, and cooked turkey meat, if using.

Grease an 8-inch cake pan. Layer the phyllo sheets in a stack, brushing each sheet with melted butter as you go. Line the inside of the pan with the phyllo pastry dough, letting the sheets hang over the sides. Fill with the rice mixture, fold the dough over the top, and brush with melted butter. Bake in a preheated 350°F oven for 25–30 minutes until golden brown. Turn onto a dish and serve hot or cold.

CDW

SIDE DISHES

Jennifer and Clarissa about to be swept away at Wandlebury Ring by Bill Clark, warden of the park.

CLARISSA WRITES: To me the making or breaking of any menu rests with the accompaniments to the main course. It is all very well to have a splendid central dish, but so often one sees the cook's concentration wavering when it comes to the vegetables. I am very lucky to have so many friends who grow their own vegetables and give me their surplus, but I have to admit it is very hard to find decent vegetables to buy. I don't know what happens to our own home-grown vegetables. We are told the growers are in thrall to the supermarkets, but if you check the shelves they are full of foreign imports, especially the unspeakable Dutch ones. I suppose somewhere in the world people are marveling at

English carrots or Scots broccoli. Now that I am back in the catering business I see the difficulty even more. I once had to go to a supermarket to buy the Jersey Royals I had put on a menu and one day the very helpful girl from Anderson's, our veg suppliers, told me a particular item had not been good enough from the market so she had gone to a supermarket for our supplies! Don't think I am weakening on supermarkets, although Jennifer has been known to visit them; their vegetables are irradiated, chilled out of existence, and tasteless, and the only thing to do with tasteless products is to use them as a base and add other flavors to them.

When designing your menu, remember that in a piece of jewelry every minor stone plays its part. There is nothing worse than bowls of unadorned vegetables untouched by butter or oil or a sprinkling of parsley or whatever. Restaurants have real problems with this and either serve you a demi-lune salad dish full of uninteresting flaccid, sad little objects or increasingly no vegetables at all save a token infant by way of garnish.

Buy the best vegetables you can, if they don't have much taste do something to them until they do, and mound your serving bowls high to give a feeling of abundance—if you do have any leftovers, you could always try making some soup with them.

Baked Beets with Sour Cream and Mint

I learned this recipe years ago from one of my greatest friends, Nandy Routh, wife of Jonathan (the original Candid Camera man). Alas, she was killed in a motor accident, but this splendid vegetable dish, originally Persian I think, always reminds me of her.

raw beets
olive oil
salt and freshly ground pepper
sour cream
finely chopped fresh mint
or good dried mint

I find the long triangular beets are best for this dish, but it really doesn't matter. Place as many of the beets as you deem necessary in a roasting pan or baking tray. Caress them with olive oil and season with salt and pepper. Bake them in a preheated oven at 400°F for about 1 hour, or until tender to the pierce of a sharp knife or skewer. To serve, split open, and add a good dollop of sour cream and a generous sprinkling of chopped mint.

JP

Gratin of Beets

I love beets, their wonderful medieval color cheering us in the gray months, their texture and sweetness, and the way they lend themselves so well to pickles and chutneys. This recipe comes from the late, great Jane Grigson's *Vegetable Book*, a volume I open every time I cook for company.

4 tablespoons (½ stick) butter
3 tablespoons grated sharp cheddar cheese
2 tablespoons grated Parmesan cheese
6 beets, boiled, skinned, and diced
salt and freshly ground pepper
6 anchovy fillets
1½ cups heavy cream
bread crumbs

Butter a gratin dish using 1 tablespoon of the butter and sprinkle one-third of the cheeses over it. Add half the beets. Season well and spread another third of the cheeses over. Lay the anchovy fillets on top and repeat with the rest of the beets and the cheeses, packing in well. Pour over enough cream to come to the top of the beets. Scatter with a few bread crumbs and dot with bits of butter.

Bake for about 15 minutes in a preheated 400°F oven until bubbling and golden brown.

CDW

Proper Bread Sauce

This much-beloved sauce can be a terrible disappointment when served in hotels and restaurants and, I'm afraid, many people's houses. The French have never seen the point of it, although I have made a few converts. It couldn't be simpler, the all-important point being the flavoring of the milk. There is never enough sauce, so make a lot. It is delicious served cold with the remains of a bird.

1 onion
10 cloves or more, to taste
2½ cups whole milk
2 tablespoons (¼ stick) butter
1 bay leaf
12–16 tablespoons fresh white bread crumbs, made from day-old good bread
1½ cups heavy cream
salt and freshly ground pepper
freshly grated nutmeg

Peel the onion and stud it with the cloves. Place it in a saucepan with the milk, butter and bay leaf. Bring to a boil, lower the heat, and simmer for 2 minutes. Remove from the heat, cover, and leave to steep all day so the milk absorb the flavors.

When nearly ready to serve, reheat the milk. Add the bread crumbs, a few tablespoons at a time until you get the right consistency, remembering they will swell. (I make the bread crumbs in a food processor, which is fast and easy.) Add the cream and season well with salt and pepper and finally with a good scraping of nutmeg. Remove the onion and bay leaf. Transfer to a well-warmed gravy boat and serve with whatever you had in mind.

JP

Hoppin' John

This very comforting dish is a classic of southern American cooking, although it probably originates from the West Indies. Eat this on its own or as an accompaniment to any meat you might fancy.

1⅓ cups dried black-eye peas
1 teaspoon salt
½ pound slab bacon, cut into lardons
1 medium onion, finely chopped
2 garlic cloves, crushed
4 tomatoes, skinned, seeded, and coarsely chopped
1 bay leaf
pinch of thyme
2 teaspoons cayenne pepper
salt and freshly ground pepper
¾ cup long-grain rice

Soak the black-eye peas overnight in cold water to cover generously. Drain the peas, put them in a saucepan with enough cold water to cover. Add the salt, bring to a boil, and boil rapidly for 10 minutes. Lower the heat and simmer for about 1 hour, or until tender.

Fry the bacon and set aside. Fry the onion and garlic until soft, but not brown, in the residual bacon fat. Add the tomatoes and fry lightly for 1 minute.

Add the onion, garlic, tomatoes, bacon, bay leaf, thyme, cayenne pepper and black pepper to the cooked black-eye peas, then taste for salt. Cook for a further 20 minutes, by which time the water should have evaporated. Meanwhile, cook the rice and drain. Add to the black-eye peas mixture and transfer to a serving dish.

JP

Fava Beans with Dill

I love fava beans, but sadly in Britain we tend to discard the pods which are sometimes better than the beans themselves. My father had many Egyptian contacts as he was involved in the setting up of the Anglo-American hospital in Cairo. He loved their food and regularly had pigeons and mullet roe sent from Cairo. His friend Dr. Halim Grace gave him this recipe.

2 pounds young fresh fava beans in their pods
⅔ cup olive oil
2 onions, chopped
2 garlic cloves, finely chopped
2 tablespoons lemon juice
½ teaspoon sugar
salt
1¼ cups boiling water
2 tablespoons freshly chopped dill
1 cup thick plain yogurt
pita breads, to serve

Wash the beans, and top, tail and string them where necessary, then set aside.

Heat the oil in a large, heavy-bottomed pan with a tight fitting cover. Sauté the onions and garlic to soften. Lower the heat, add the beans, in their pods, the lemon juice, sugar, and salt to taste. Stir and stew gently for 15 minutes, stirring occasionally. Add the water and half the dill, adjust to a gentle simmer, and cook for 1 hour until the pods are very tender. Leave to cool.

Pour the lot into a dish with the rest of the dill. Serve with the yogurt and hot pita bread. This dish improves with keeping.

CDW

Fava Bean Pod Purée

This is another delicious way of using the fava bean pods, which you may normally throw away. The purée is very good with ham, and you can enclose some in a slice to make an interesting canapé or cold buffet dish.

2 pounds fava bean pods
water
salt and freshly ground pepper
1 tablespoon butter

Top and tail your pods and simmer in a large pan of salted water until they are tender, about 20–30 minutes depending on their age. Drain and either put through the food mill or purée in a blender or food processor. Season and reheat with the butter.

CDW

Cauliflower with Almond Sauce

This is a Spanish recipe and makes an interesting change to the more-usual white sauce. The tip about the bay leaf is one of the most useful things the Cordon Bleu taught me; be careful not to throw it away until you have drained the cauliflower.

1 medium cauliflower
1 bay leaf
2 tablespoons (¼ stick) butter
5½ tablespoons all-purpose flour
1¼ cups milk
2 tablespoons finely ground blanched almonds
½ teaspoon chili powder
salt
toasted slivered almonds, to serve

Cook the cauliflower with the bay leaf to prevent odor.

Melt the butter, stir in the flour, and gradually add the milk, then the almonds, chili powder, and salt to taste. Cook until the sauce thickens, stirring for 1 minute or more. If the sauce is too thick add more milk.

Put the cauliflower in a serving dish and pour the sauce over. Sprinkle with toasted almond flakes and serve.

CDW

Sardinian Artichoke Pie

Globe artichokes are very Elizabethan. They don't grow too well in Britain, so I snap them up whenever I see them. Out of season, they are good in jars, and any delicatessen worth its salt should have them. This makes a good vegetarian main course as well as an excellent supper dish.

28 artichoke hearts or 12 baby artichokes
1½ cups fresh white bread crumbs
2 cups grated Parmesan cheese
2 cups grated Romano cheese
3 tablespoons drained capers, chopped
½ pound ripe olives, pitted and halved
5 medium tomatoes, skinned and thinly sliced, or 1 large can plum tomatoes, drained and chopped
10 ounces Fontina or Gruyère cheese, thinly sliced
3 tablespoons olive oil

If using whole baby artichokes, trim the leaves, and boil the artichokes until tender. Drain and slice thinly.

Butter a 10-inch springform cake pan and coat with one-third of the bread crumbs. In a bowl, mix together the Parmesan, Romano, and the remaining bread crumbs. Arrange layers in the cake pan, beginning with the artichokes, followed by the capers and olives, tomatoes, Fontina, and then the bread crumb mixture. Drizzle 1 tablespoon of olive oil over this and repeat, pressing down well. These quantities should make three layers.

Bake in a preheated 350°F oven for 25 minutes. Leave to cool for 10 minutes, unmold, and serve with a salad.

CDW

Broccoli with Corn and Chorizo Sauce

Like the former American President George Bush, I am not that fond of broccoli, although I love purple sprouting variety. However it is sometimes the only green vegetable around and this recipe is a good way of enlivening it. If you want to make it more substantial, add more chorizo sausage and have it as a supper dish.

1½ pounds broccoli
½ cup (1 stick) butter
4 shallots, chopped
3 cups corn kernels
2 tablespoons water
pinch of grated nutmeg
4 ounces chorizo sausage, chopped
salt and freshly ground pepper

Separate the broccoli into flowerets. Melt 4 tablespoons (½ stick) of the butter in a pan. Add the broccoli and stir to coat with butter. Add water to cover and cook for about 5 minutes, or until just tender, but still crunchy.

In another pan, melt the remaining 4 tablespoons (½ stick) of the butter. Add the shallots and corn and cook until the shallots are soft. Blend this mixture together in a food processor, adding a little water. Return to the pan, add the nutmeg, sausage, and salt and pepper. Gently heat through. Thin if too thick and pour over the broccoli.

CDW

Tomato Tart

A tomato tart looks wonderful with its dramatic colors. This is really a leftover salade Niçoise that I put into a pie crust one day. If you use a piece of fresh tuna it is even better and more sophisticated.

FOR THE PIE CRUST DOUGH:
¾ cup plus 1 tablespoon all-purpose flour
2 tablespoons (¼ stick) butter
2 tablespoons lard or vegetable shortening
1 tablespoon freshly grated Parmesan cheese (optional)
salt
cold water

FOR THE FILLING:
1 pound tomatoes
2 tablespoons olive oil
1 medium onion, finely chopped
1 garlic clove, finely chopped
1 teaspoon oregano
salt and freshly ground pepper
6 anchovy fillets, chopped, or 1 small can of tuna, or 4-ounce piece of fresh tuna
2 tablespoons grated sharp cheddar cheese
2 large eggs
⅔ cup light cream
2 tablespoons pitted black olives, chopped

To make the pie crust, sift the flour and salt together. Cut in the butter and lard until the mixture resembles fine bread crumbs. Add the cheese and bind with a little cold water. Chill for at least 30 minutes. Roll out the pastry dough on a lightly floured surface and use to line an 8-inch quiche dish. Chill again for 30 minutes. Line the pie shell with aluminum foil and baking beans and bake blind in a preheated 400°F oven for 10 minutes. Remove the foil and beans and bake for a further 5 minutes.

Skin, seed and slice the tomatoes, straining and reserving the juice. In a small pan, heat the oil over low heat and sauté the onion until soft. Add the garlic and oregano and cook for 1 minute. Add the tomato juice and salt and pepper, and cook until the juice is almost absorbed. Put this in the pastry case and cover with fish. (If you are using fresh tuna cook it in a pan with a little more oil for about 2 minutes, turning as necessary, then flake it.) Cover with tomatoes and grated cheese. Whisk the eggs with the cream and pour over the tomatoes, scattering the olives on top.

Bake in a preheated 400°F oven for 20-25 minutes, or until the filling has set. Serve hot or cold with a green salad, or a salad of green beans, or deep-fried green beans which you have dipped in batter.

CDW

Illustrated overleaf

Green Beans with Bacon and Tomato

A variation on the ever-popular green bean. This can be used as a side dish or even as a first course, or as an addition to pasta.

6 ounces slab bacon, diced
1½ cups stock
1½ pounds green beans
5 medium tomatoes, skinned, seeded, and coarsely chopped
salt and fresh ground pepper
1 tablespoon chopped parsley

Put the bacon and stock into a pan and bring to a boil. Lower the heat and simmer the bacon for 20 minutes. Add the beans, tomatoes, and pepper. Taste for salt as it should not be necessary to add any unless the bacon is very mild. Bring back to a boil. Lower the heat and simmer until the beans are tender.

Strain the beans, bacon, and tomatoes into a serving dish. The beans may lose a bit of color but their flavor will be enhanced. Sprinkle with parsley and serve.

JP

Swiss Chard with Garlic and Anchovies

I adore Swiss chard and it grew very profusely on the pheasant farm where I cooked. This is a good way of using the stalks.

2 pounds Swiss chard, with white stalks
2 tablespoons olive oil
4 garlic cloves
1 small can anchovies
freshly ground black pepper

Wash the chard. Cut off the white stalks and trim their ends and any discolored portions. Heat the oil in a covered pan. Add the garlic and anchovies and cook until the anchovies melt into the oil, about 5 minutes.

Cut the chard stalks into 1-inch pieces, and blanch them in boiling water. Refresh under cold water and drain well. Add them to the oil and season with the pepper. Cover and cook gently for 10 minutes. If you wish you may add the chard greens at this stage and cook for a further 3–5 minutes, or you may wish to use the greens for something else.

CDW

Couscous Salad

Couscous seems to be appearing everywhere these days, so voilà.

1½ cups couscous
1 red bell pepper, skinned, seeded, and chopped
1 yellow bell pepper, skinned, seeded, and chopped
4 scallions, finely chopped
3 tomatoes, skinned, seeded, and chopped
1 tablespoon chopped parsley
1 tablespoon chopped olives

FOR THE DRESSING:
¼ cup virgin olive oil
grated zest and juice of ½ lemon
1 garlic clove, crushed
salt and freshly ground pepper

Cook the couscous according to the directions on the package. When the grains have swollen, fold in the salad ingredients.

Put the dressing ingredients in a covered jar and shake vigorously. Pour over the couscous and mix well before turning into a serving dish.

JP

Hot Curried Cabbage

During the winter when there is a poor variety of fresh vegetables and a lot of cabbage, this makes an interesting way of dealing with that estimable, if somewhat dull, vegetable.

½ large cabbage, shredded
1 cup stock
1 bay leaf
2 garlic cloves
2 cloves
1 onion
all-purpose flour
salt and freshly ground pepper
1 tablespoon curry powder
3 tablespoons (⅜ stick) butter
½ cup light cream
½ cup dried bread crumbs

Put the cabbage in a large pan and add the stock, bay leaf and garlic. Stick the cloves into the onion and add to the cabbage. Cook over medium heat for 10 minutes. Drain the cabbage and discard the bay leaf and the onion.

Put the cabbage into a greased baking dish. Mix together the curry powder, half the butter, and salt and pepper, add the cream and stir until smooth. Pour over the cabbage. Sprinkle with the bread crumbs and dot with the remaining butter. Bake in a preheated 350°F oven for 20 minutes.

CDW

Jerusalem Artichokes with Fine Herbs

This is a delicious vegetable dish, particularly good with poultry or even game. I love it, although its disadvantage is that it tends to create quite a lot of wind, but never mind.

1 pound Jerusalem artichokes, peeled and rinsed
salt and freshly ground pepper
2 shallots, finely chopped
1 garlic clove, finely chopped
2 tablespoons (¼ stick) butter
1 tablespoon all-purpose flour
1¼ cups milk
pinch of grated nutmeg
½ tablespoon chopped chives
1 tablespoon chopped parsley

Cut the artichokes into evenly sized pieces, cover with water in a saucepan, add 1 teaspoon of salt, and bring to the boil. Lower the heat and simmer for about 30 minutes. Check to see if they are cooked, then strain.

Meanwhile, melt the butter in a saucepan. Add the shallots and garlic and gently fry until they are soft, but not colored. Stir in the flour with a wooden spoon. Add the milk gradually, stirring constantly, then add the grated nutmeg. When the sauce has thickened to a nice consistency add ¼ teaspoon of pepper, the chives and most of the parsley. Stir into the artichokes. Sprinkle the remaining parsley over the whole mixture.

JP

Mushrooms with Chicken Livers

When I was young chicken livers were an enormous treat, and I still think of them as such. Luckily they are freely available nowadays. It is terribly important to keep the little livers pink on the inside, otherwise they will become tough and crumbly. Always make sure the bile duct is removed.

1 medium onion, thinly sliced
1 garlic clove, crushed
2 tablespoons (¼ stick) butter
1 tablespoon olive oil
6 cups sliced mushrooms
½ pound chicken livers
salt and freshly ground pepper
1¼ cups dry white wine
¼ cup balsamic vinegar
1 tablespoon chopped parsley
hot toast, to serve

Fry the onion and garlic in the butter and oil until they are lightly colored. Add the mushrooms and fry until they are softened. Chop the chicken livers into bite-size pieces and add to the mushrooms. Cook for about 3–4 minutes and season with salt and pepper.

Put the wine and balsamic vinegar in a saucepan and boil to reduce by half. Add the chopped parsley. Pour over the chicken livers. Serve with hot toast.

JP

Stuffed Onion Rolls

This is a Saudi Arabian dish and was adapted from a curious book, *Memory Recipes of Desert Storm*, which was published following the Gulf War. I met the author, Monica Gabur, and it is the only time I have ever tried to negotiate with someone in full purdah. Not easy I can tell you. The recipe is a bit fiddly but worth the effort, unlike another recipe 'Lamp feet with toes' which turned out to be lamb's trotters with toast!

4 large onions
1 teaspoon ground cinnamon
½ teaspoon ground allspice
1 pound ground lamb
7 ounces tomatoes, chopped
3 tablespoons dried bread crumbs
1 tablespoon chopped parsley
salt and freshly ground pepper
1 teaspoon sugar
juice of ½ lemon
1 tablespoon oil

Peel the onions carefully and cut off the root ends. Make a single slit in each onion from top to bottom being careful not to slice the onion all the way through but to leave one half intact. Put in a saucepan of boiling water and simmer for 10 minutes. Drain, cool and separate carefully into layers.

Mix together the cinnamon, allspice, lamb, tomatoes and bread crumbs. Add the parsley and salt and pepper. Place 1 tablespoon of the stuffing on each onion slice and roll up tightly. Line the bottom of a heavy-bottomed saucepan with the unused onion pieces. Pack in the rolls closely, seam side down. Mix the sugar and lemon juice with ½ cup of water and pour over the rolls. Top with the oil.

Place a small upturned saucer or plate over the onions to prevent unrolling. Simmer gently over a low heat for 1 hour, adding water if necessary. Transfer to a serving plate.

CDW

Peas with Lettuce

Test the peas occasionally for taste and tenderness. I often add chopped scallions to this recipe, but this is optional.

6 tablespoons (¾ stick) butter
5 cups fresh shelled peas
2 small lettuce hearts, tied up with string
1 bouquet garni
1½ teaspoons salt
2 teaspoons sugar
3 tablespoons water
⅔ cup heavy cream

Melt the butter in a saucepan. Add the peas, lettuce hearts, bouquet garni, salt, sugar, and water. Simmer with the lid on for 40 minutes.

Remove the lettuces and drain the peas, reserving the liquid. The amount of liquid should be very little but reduce it to about 2 tablespoonfuls. Whisk in the cream and pour over the peas. Cut the lettuce hearts into quarters and place on the peas.

JP

Salad of Lettuce Hearts

Make sure your hearts are nice and firm and you won't go wrong with this simple salad.

Some good lettuce hearts
bunch of watercress
bunch of salad cress or
mustardcress
1 hard-boiled egg

FOR THE DRESSING:
¼ cup virgin olive oil
1 tablespoon wine vinegar
salt and freshly ground pepper

Arrange the lettuce hearts in a salad bowl and sprinkle with finely chopped watercress leaves and cut cress. (If salad or mustard cress is not available, increase the quantity of watercress.) Separate the white of the egg from the yolk and push both through a fine strainer. Sprinkle over the salad.

Put the ingredients for the dressing in a covered jar and shake vigorously. Pour over the salad just before serving.

JP

Spinach and Rice

A great comfort, and so good for you, too.

2 tablespoons virgin olive oil
4 shallots, finely chopped
1 large garlic clove, chopped
¾ cup long-grain rice, cooked
6 ounces spinach, cooked, drained, and puréed
1 tablespoon finely chopped mint
½ teaspoon ground cinnamon
salt and freshly ground pepper

Heat the olive oil in a skillet. Add the shallots and garlic and cook for a few minutes until soft, but not brown. Add the rice to the skillet, stir, and coat with the oil. Add the spinach, mint, cinnamon, and salt and pepper and stir. Cook until the contents of the pan are heated through.

JP

Pete's Pommy Pommes

This comes from a magnificent Australian friend, Pete Smith, and my nickname for them is Pommy Pommes. Pete served them at a dinner party with roast lamb, but I have used them with game where they are perfect and easier than proper game chips. Not enough is made of potatoes, and I think everyone would love this crunchy, succulent method.

1 pound waxy potatoes, peeled
olive oil
⅔ cup vegetable or chicken stock
salt and freshly ground pepper
herbs of your choice (parsley, thyme, tarragon, etc.)
4 garlic cloves, finely chopped

Slice the potatoes very finely on a mandolin, with a good, sharp knife, or in a food processor. Soak in cold water for 30 minutes. Drain and pat dry.

Drizzle some olive oil over the bottom of a roasting pan. (There should only be about 5 layers of potatoes, so choose your roasting pan accordingly.) Put a layer of overlapping potato slices on the bottom of the pan, season with salt and pepper, add a sprinkling of herbs and garlic, and a drizzle of olive oil, then moisten with a little stock. Continue in this manner until everything is used up.

Place in a preheated 375°F oven until softish when pierced. Increase the heat to 450°F and continue cooking until very brown and crisp. Serve with what you will.

JP

Potato Dumplings with Chanterelles

Chanterelles grow freely in Scotland, indeed there were so many last year that my friends Charles and Anne Fraser sent me a box by post from their Highland retreat. Some people make the mistake of using too strong flavors with these delicate mushrooms, but this dish suits them very well. It is an excellent accompaniment to roast meat or stews and a good supper dish on its own.

1½ pounds potatoes, peeled
¾ cup and 1 tablespoon all-purpose flour
1 egg
1 egg yolk
salt and freshly ground pepper
⅔ cup cottage cheese
5 ounces chanterelles or other wild mushrooms
4 tablespoons (½ stick) butter
3 shallots, minced
melted butter for brushing

Boil and mash the potatoes. Mix in the flour, egg, egg yolk and salt to taste and allow the heat from the mashed potatoes to cook the eggs. Press the cheese through a strainer, and drain off any excess liquid. Clean and chop the mushrooms. Melt the butter and sauté the mushrooms with the shallots. Leave the mushrooms and shallots to cool slightly, then stir in the strained cheese.

Roll the potato into a sausage and cut into sixteen equal portions. Roll each portion into a ball. Make an indentation in each ball and stuff with the mushroom mixture, pinching the potato around the filling to seal it.

Bring a large pan of salted water to a boil. Add the dumplings and poach them for 10 minutes. Drain well and leave to cool.

Heat the broiler. Brush each dumpling with a little melted butter and broil until brown.

CDW

Sugar-Browned Potatoes

This is a different way of serving new potatoes and is particularly good with the tasteless new potatoes you buy out of season or you know where! Do not, for instance, waste Jersey Royals on this recipe. It is also a good way for reheating cooked leftover new potatoes.

2 pounds new potatoes
4 tablespoons (½ stick) butter
2 tablespoons sugar

Scrub the potatoes to remove any dirt and cook until tender. Do not under- or overcook, either is a crime.

In a heavy pan, melt the butter. Add the sugar and cook over a low heat until the sugar begins to caramelize. Add the potatoes and make sure they become well coated in the caramel. Continue this process until the caramel is a good, rich brown. Serve at once.

CDW

PUDDINGS (DESSERTS) AND CAKES

Picnicking in Cambridge.

CLARISSA WRITES: Many a bad meal has been saved by a good pudding (dessert). It is the last thing one goes away remembering and sometimes, when a meal is consistently bad, you find yourself waiting for the bought ice cream you know will inevitably follow. I think of the puddings we have served on the program over the series and how well they have been received. It is good to make a pudding especially to fit, like Jennifer's Peaches Cardinal Hume for the priests at Westminster Cathedral. But one must avoid the danger of falling into the trap of becoming like an Edwardian chef and naming every pudding for one's friends.

Another approach to puddings is an adaptation of the familiar to surprise, like my Christmas Pudding Ice Cream Bombe, which I made for the Winchester choirboys on our first Christmas special. To digress slightly, due to the constraints of time I was not allowed the easier intermittent step of freezing the two halves of the bombe before inserting the brandy butter (hard sauce) center and closing the bombe. "Slap it together," said Pat Llewellyn, our wild Welsh producer. With an over-heated Aga behind me and the arc lamps heating the air in front, my bombe was melting rapidly, and I was acutely conscious that had my aim missed, the bishop would have had to redecorate his kitchen.

My friend Angus Hamilton is so fond of ice cream that he loaned me the vintage ice-cream maker I used at Winchester, so in return I might design an ice cream for him; testing is still in progress. One friend, a recovering alcoholic like me, desperately missed eating trifle, so I had the interesting chore of designing a sherry-free trifle, which I finally achieved with a mixture of orange juice and balsamic vinegar!

Almond and Semolina Custard

Even at school, where I was scorned for it, I liked semolina, and, as an adult, I like this pudding for its subtle sophisticated flavor. I have weaned many people from their childhood aversion with this dish, so do try it please.

2 tablespoons (¼ stick) butter
1 cup slivered, blanched almonds
6 ounces fine semolina
1 cup plus 1 tablespoon sugar
1 quart milk
1 teaspoon grated lemon zest
ground cinnamon

Melt the butter gently in a saucepan. Toss in the almonds and fry until they begin to color. Add the semolina and stir until it begins to color.

In another pan, dissolve the sugar in the milk and bring to a boil. Add the lemon zest. Pour the milk over the semolina and almonds, and stir constantly until it thickens. Continue cooking for a further 1 minute. Pour the mixture onto saucers, sprinkle with cinnamon, and serve warm.

CDW

Peasant Girl with Veil

Not a dish for the average peasant girl, I wouldn't think, except maybe in Normandy. There she could find her apples and her Calvados, which can be used instead of brandy, and good luck to her.

2 heaped tablespoons whole-wheat bread crumbs
4 tablespoons (½ stick) butter
1½ pounds apples, peeled, cored, and sliced
scant 2 tablespoons brown sugar
1 tablespoon brandy
1 cup heavy cream, whipped
4 ounces bittersweet chocolate, grated

Fry the bread crumbs in the butter until golden brown. Cook the apples with the brown sugar in a little water and, when cooked, stir in the brandy.

In a glass dish, arrange alternate layers of bread crumbs and apples, finishing with a layer of bread crumbs. Cover the top layer with the whipped cream and sprinkle the grated chocolate over the top.

JP

Apple Balls

This is a Dutch recipe given to me by my Dutch godmother. You should not use cooking apples as they are purely a Victorian English invention and are designed to collapse. For this dish you need fruit that will keep its shape.

heaping 3¾ cups all-purpose flour
pinch of salt
¾ cup (1½ sticks) unsalted butter
2 eggs
½ cup sour cream
6 apples
2 tablespoons sugar
2 teaspoons ground cinnamon
½ cup golden raisins
2 tablespoons (¼ stick) butter

Sift the flour and salt into a bowl. Cut in the unsalted butter to the crumb stage. Beat together 1 egg and the sour cream and add to the flour. Mix to form a dough and knead. Cover in plastic wrap and chill for 30 minutes.

Peel and core the apples. Mix together the sugar, cinnamon, and golden raisins. Stuff each apple with a little of the sugar mixture and add a small piece of butter.

Roll out the pastry dough on a lightly floured surface. Cut into six squares each large enough to enclose an apple. Wrap each apple in its pastry dough overcoat, lightly beat the remaining egg and use to bind the seam. Place on a greased baking sheet and bake in a preheated 375°F oven until golden brown, about 30 minutes.

CDW

Apple Strudel

You will find this famous national dish in every cake shop and café in Austria and Germany, not to mention Soho in London. Don't be frightened by the phyllo pastry—it is quite easy to manage as long as you keep it moist. I prefer to use Bramley apples for strudel.

1 pound cooking apples, peeled, cored, and cut into thin slices
¼ cup superfine sugar
½ teaspoon ground cinnamon
¼ cup golden raisins
¼ cup finely chopped walnuts
1 teaspoon grated lemon zest
8 sheets phyllo dough
6 tablespoons (¾ stick) butter, melted
2 tablespoons fresh white bread crumbs

In a mixing bowl, combine the apples, sugar, cinnamon, golden raisins, walnuts, and lemon zest. Keep the phyllo dough covered with a damp cloth to prevent it drying out.

Lay a sheet of the phyllo dough on a damp cloth, brush with melted butter, and cover with a thin layer of bread crumbs. Put another sheet of phyllo dough on top and repeat the process once more. Arrange a 1-inch thick roll of apple mixture 2 inches from the longest end of the phyllo dough nearest to you. Lift up the end of the damp cloth nearest you and the phyllo dough will begin to roll over. Roll the phyllo dough over the apple mixture, and continue to roll to get a Swiss roll effect. Repeat with the rest of the phyllo dough and apple mixture.

Bake in a preheated 425°F oven for 10 minutes. Lower the heat to 400°F and bake for a further 20 minutes, or until the strudel is crisp and brown.

JP

Quercyan Apple Cake

Usually I keep my recipes very simple but this, though somewhat harder than usual, really repays the effort. Most of my stay in Quercy is either unremembered or censored, but the recipe remains.

FOR THE FILLING:
3 pounds apples, peeled and thinly sliced
1 cup plus 2 tablespoons sugar
½ cup rum
6 tablespoons orange flower-water
thinly pared zest of 1 lemon

3¼ cups all-purpose flour
½ teaspoon baking powder
2 eggs
3 tablespoons (⅜ stick) butter, creamed

TO FINISH:
2 tablespoons (¼ stick) butter, melted
1 egg, beaten
superfine sugar

Macerate the sliced apples with the other filling ingredients overnight. Strain the apples, reserving the juice.

Sift the flour and baking powder into a large bowl and make a well in the middle. Add the butter and egg and working with your fingertips, gradually add ¾ cup plus 2 tablespoons of the liquid from the apples. Work into a smooth and elastic paste with your hand. Leave to rest for 2 hours.

Roll out the paste as thinly as possible, then transfer to a floured cloth on a large table. Working from the middle, with the palms of your hands, carefully stretch the paste to the thinness of a cigarette paper. Rest it and yourself for 1 hour.

Brush lightly with melted butter and dust with sugar. Cover with well drained apples and roll up. Mix the remaining juice into the beaten egg and brush over the top. Bake in a preheated 400°F oven for 50–55 minutes.

CDW

Apricot Mousse

You will certainly feel like the tipsy pussycat who has got the cream after consuming this delectable mousse.

½ pound dried apricots
½ cup water
¼ cup sugar
1 tablespoon orange-flavored liqueur, or brandy
few drops of vanilla extract
½ cup heavy cream, whipped
2 tablespoons blanched, slivered almonds
fancy cookies, such as Langue de Chat

Place the apricots in a saucepan and add ½ cup of water or just enough to cover the fruit. Add the sugar and bring to a boil. Lower the heat and simmer for about 30 minutes.

Remove the apricots from the heat and purée them with the remaining liquid. Add the liqueur and the vanilla extract and fold in the cream and almonds.

Spoon into individual glasses and chill. Before serving sprinkle with a few more slivered almonds, another blob of cream, and add the cookies.

JP

Cheese and Honey Pie

The Greeks love honey sweet desserts. This one may not be to everybody's taste, but goes well with the addition of a tart fruit salad on the side.

4 ounces refrigerated ready-made pie crust
1 cup low-fat cheese, such as ricotta
3 tablespoons honey
2 eggs, well beaten
juice of ½ lemon
1 teaspoon ground cinnamon
1 cup walnuts, crushed

Line an 8-inch quiche dish with the pie crust dough. Line with aluminum foil and baking beans and bake blind in a preheated 350°F oven for 10 minutes. Remove the pie shell from the oven and increase the heat to 375°F. Meanwhile, mix the cheese with the honey. Add the eggs, lemon juice, and half the cinnamon and mix thoroughly. Cover the pastry base with walnuts and pour the filling mixture on top. Return the pie to the oven and bake for 30 minutes. Make sure the filling is set and then sprinkle the remaining cinnamon on top.

JP

Hot Chocolate Soufflés

Nobody can resist a chocolate soufflé unless they're allergic. You can make just one large soufflé, in which case it will take about 30 minutes to cook.

3 ounces good-quality
bittersweet chocolate
1 tablespoon brandy or rum
2 tablespoons (¼ stick) butter
2 tablespoons all-purpose
flour
⅔ cup milk
⅓ cup superfine sugar
½ teaspoon vanilla extract
4 eggs, separated

Break up the chocolate and put it into a bowl with the brandy or rum. Put the bowl over a saucepan of gently simmering water and allow to melt slowly, stirring.

Melt the butter in another saucepan. Add the flour and cook over low heat for a few minutes, stirring constantly. Warm the milk in another pan. Dissolve the sugar in the milk and then blend into the flour and butter. Continue to cook slowly, stirring constantly, until the mixture thickens.

Remove the saucepan from the heat. Add the vanilla extract and chocolate mixture and mix well. Add the lightly beaten egg yolks and beat well. Whisk the egg whites fairly stiffly and then fold into the chocolate mixture.

Spoon the mixture into four individual buttered ramekin dishes. Bake in a preheated oven at 375°F for about 15 minutes, or until the soufflés are well risen. Serve immediately.

JP

Chocolate Crème Brûlée

Everybody loves crème brûlée, and some people are seriously addicted to chocolate. I dedicate this recipe to Rebekka Hardy, who not only made me a better cook, but also made me think about chocolate 24 hours a day.

2½ cups heavy cream
1 vanilla bean, split
11 ounces semisweet chocolate
4 medium egg yolks
½ cup confectioners' sugar, sifted
3 tablespoons superfine sugar

In a heavy-bottomed saucepan, heat the cream with the vanilla bean until scalding hot, but not boiling. Remove from the heat, cover, and leave to infuse for 15 minutes.

Remove the bean and scrape the seeds into the cream with the tip of a knife. Break up the chocolate and stir it into the cream until melted and smooth.

Put the egg yolks and confectioners' sugar into a bowl. Beat with a wooden spoon until well blended. Stir in the chocolate cream. Pour into four individual ramekin dishes. Arrange the ramekins in a baking dish and add hot water to come halfway up the sides of the ramekins. Bake in a preheated 350°F oven for 30 minutes until firm. Remove and cool. Chill overnight, or for up to 48 hours.

Sprinkle superfine sugar over the top and put under a hot broiler to caramelize. Serve within 1 hour.

CDW

Chocolate Egg Snowball

This is a variation on what I call *oafs à la neigh*. I once had a dearly loved employer who was addicted to chocolate. "It's just like your gin, dear," she would say as she sent me to the village store at midnight. I spent a lot of time adapting recipes to include chocolate!

4 ounces semisweet chocolate
6 eggs, separated
2 tablespoons superfine sugar
1 quart whole milk
½ cup granulated sugar

Melt the chocolate over hot water. Beat the egg whites until very stiff. Add the 2 tablespoons of the superfine sugar and whisk again until stiff and the sugar dissolves. Bring the milk to a simmer in a wide, flat pan. Shape the egg white mass into a round, flat cake, and poach this gently in the simmering milk for a few minutes. Turn it carefully with a pancake turner and poach the other side. Leave to drain on paper towels or a clean cloth.

Beat the egg yolks and half the granulated sugar into the melted chocolate. Pour the slightly cooled milk over the mixture. Place over hot (not boiling) water in the top of a double boiler. Cook, stirring constantly, until the mixture thickens to the consistency of thin cream. Pour into a glass bowl and place the egg whites on top. Chill.

Ten minutes before serving, heat the remaining sugar in a heavy-bottomed saucepan until it caramelizes to a golden brown and pour over the egg whites.

CDW

Coconut Blancmange with Cranberry Sauce

A pale and interesting dessert with a dramatic red sauce. Even those who dread the word blancmange will like the coconut effect, I hope. My various sojourns in the West Indies have left me with a taste for the fruit and a large supply of recipes.

12 ounces shredded
unsweetened coconut
5 cups milk
6 tablespoons cornstarch
½ cup superfine sugar
⅔ cup cranberries
¼ cup granulated sugar
juice of ½ lemon

Put the coconut and milk in a saucepan and heat to a simmering point. Remove from the heat and leave to stand for 30 minutes for the flavor to infuse. Strain through cheesecloth, pressing to extract all the liquid.

Put the cornstarch in a large bowl and blend to a smooth paste with some of the coconut-flavored milk. Put the rest of the coconut-flavored milk and superfine sugar in a pan and heat gently until the sugar dissolves. Bring to a boil and pour quickly over the cornstarch, stirring briskly. Return to the heat and stir until large bubbles break the surface.

Pour into a wetted mold and leave to cool to room temperature. To serve, chill and unmold. Heat the cranberries with the granulated sugar and lemon juice until they pop, then pour the sauce over the blancmange before serving.

CDW

Zuppa Inglese

This curious Italian name, making you think of soup, is, in fact, a good old-fashioned English trifle, far removed from the sort of thing you used to get in the nursery. The Italians took it to their hearts and have loved it ever since.

4 egg yolks
4 tablespoons sugar
1 teaspoon vanilla extract
¼ cup all-purpose flour, sifted
tiny pinch of salt
2½ cups milk
3 ounces semisweet chocolate, grated
⅔ cup Marsala
1 sponge cake, sliced crosswise into three layers

Put the egg yolks in a bowl. Gradually add the sugar and vanilla extract and beat until creamy. Add the flour, salt and ⅔ cup of the milk. Scald the remaining milk, pour it onto the mixture in the bowl, stir well, and return to the saucepan. Simmer gently, stirring constantly for about 3–4 minutes. Pour one-third of the mixture into a bowl. Add two-thirds of the grated chocolate and stir until the chocolate melts. Leave both mixtures to cool.

Place a layer of sponge cake in a serving bowl. Sprinkle with Marsala and cover with half of the plain custard. Add another layer of sponge, more Marsala, and cover with the chocolate custard. Add the last layer of sponge, sprinkle with Marsala, and cover with the remaining plain custard. Chill. Before serving, sprinkle the remaining chocolate over the custard to decorate.

JP

Omelet Stephanie

Everyone knows of the Austrian Crown Prince Rudolph and his suicide pact with his mistress Maria Vetsera at Mayerling. There have been plays, novels, and even a ballet on the theme. Prince Rudolph had a wife, the Crown Princess Stephanie, whose legacy is this delicious soufflé omelet.

2 tablespoons (¼ stick) butter
3 egg yolks
3 tablespoons confectioner's sugar, plus extra for sprinkling
3 tablespoons heavy cream
2 level tablespoons all-purpose flour
4 egg whites, stiffly beaten
6 ounces raspberries

Melt the butter in a flameproof dish, and turn the dish to spread the butter evenly. Beat the egg yolks with 2 tablespoons of the confectioners' sugar until the mixture is pale and forms ribbons. Beat in the cream and the flour, then fold this mixture into the egg whites. Slide carefully into the hot, buttered dish. Cook in a pre-heated oven at 375°F for just over 15 minutes.

Roll your raspberries in 1 tablespoon of the confectioners' sugar. Slide the omelet onto a warm plate, put the raspberries on one side, and fold over the omelet. Sprinkle with the remaining confectioners' sugar and serve at once.

CDW

Plum Kuchen

This German delight is full of cream and plums, and is very good with a cup of excellent coffee.

¾ cup plus 1 tablespoon wholewheat flour
pinch of baking powder
6 tablespoons (¾ stick) butter, softened
¼ cup blanched almonds, finely ground
heaping ½ cup brown sugar, packed
1 tablespoon ground cinnamon
1½ pounds ripe plums, cut in half and pitted
2 egg yolks
⅔ cup sour cream

Sift the flour and baking powder into a bowl. Cut in the butter, add the almonds and two-thirds of the brown sugar, and stir until well blended. Press the mixture firmly into a buttered 8–9-inch tart pan with a removeable bottom. Arrange the plums, flesh side down, to cover the mixture closely. Sprinkle with the cinnamon and the remaining sugar. Bake in a preheated 375°F oven for 20–25 minutes.

In the meanwhile, beat the egg yolks with the sour cream. When the plums come out of the oven, pour this mixture over the plums. Return to the oven and bake for a further 40 minutes, at the same temperature.

JP

Rich Vanilla Ice Cream with Chocolate Puffs

My Belgian great aunt, whose measurement around her waist when she married equalled the measurement around her neck when she died at the age of ninety-two, prided herself on her vanilla ice cream. I think you will enjoy it too.

FOR THE ICE CREAM:
1½ cups whole milk
6 tablespoons superfine sugar
1 vanilla bean, cut in half lengthwise
5 egg yolks
¾ cup heavy cream

FOR THE CHOCOLATE PUFFS:
4 ounces semisweet chocolate
2¼ cups superfine sugar
8 egg whites

In a medium saucepan, combine the milk, half the sugar, and the vanilla bean and heat to just below the boiling point; set aside for at least 15 minutes to infuse. In a heatproof bowl, mix the egg yolks and the rest of the sugar, beating, preferably with an electric mixer, until they reach the ribbon stage. Still beating, pour on the infused milk.

Now either place the bowl over boiling water or transfer the whole lot to the top of a double boiler. Stirring frequently, cook until the custard coats the back of a spoon and holds a clear line. Remove from the heat and immediately plunge the bottom of the pan into cold water to arrest the cooking process. Transfer to a bowl, cover, and refrigerate till quite cool. Add the cream and mix well. Remove the vanilla bean, scrape out the seeds, and add to the mixture, discarding the bean.

At this stage, if you have an ice-cream maker, churn the mixture for 15 minutes. If not, transfer to the freezer, stirring every 10 minutes until it is set. Serve with raspberries or other fresh fruit.

This chocolate cookie recipe is, I think, the first and comes from my Patrick Lamb, which I bought myself at Sotheby's to celebrate my tenth sober birthday. Melt the chocolate over hot water until it is soft and stir in the sugar. Mix the egg whites with a fork (do not beat them) and add to the chocolate and sugar to form a paste. Roll into pieces the size of walnuts. Place in tiny paper cups on a baking sheet covered with greased waxed paper. Bake in a preheated 275°F oven until crisp.

CDW

Christmas Pudding Ice Cream Bombe

This is the pudding I made for the Winchester choirboys in our first Christmas special. It is a lot easier to make if you are allowed to freeze each half when you have put the ice cream in, but before you add the hard-sauce center, but then you won't have a perfectionist Welsh television producer in your kitchen.

1½ cups milk
scant ½ cup brown sugar, packed
3 egg yolks
¾ cup heavy cream, chilled
1 tablespoon brandy
6 ounces steamed store-bought Christmas pudding, chopped
2 tablespoons hard sauce
1 tablespoon brandy, to serve

Put the milk and half the sugar in a medium saucepan and bring to just below the boiling point. Put the egg yolks and remaining sugar in a bowl and beat until pale and forming ribbons. Bring the milk back to a boil and pour in a thin stream onto the egg yolks and sugar, whisking steadily. Pour into the top of a double boiler and stir the custard until it thickens to form a clear line when coating the back of a spoon. Plunge the bottom of the pan into cold water. Transfer the custard to a bowl, cover and chill. When the custard is cold, pour in the chilled cream.

Stir the brandy into the custard and churn in an ice-cream maker until it is the consistency of whipped cream. If you do not have an ice-cream maker, transfer to the freezer, stirring every 10 minutes. Crumble in the pudding and churn for a further 5 seconds. Scrape into a freezerproof container and freeze for 1-2 hours.

Place four individual metal pudding molds into the freezer to chill. Divide the custard mixture equally between the chilled bombe molds and freeze. Top up the molds with the hard sauce and close the bombe. Allow to freeze hard. Turn out, pour the brandy over and ignite.

CDW

181

Rhum Babas

This is an outrageously sticky pudding, soaked in rum and covered in syrup—a good heart stopper.
It was one of my mother's favorite delicacies and she lived to eighty-eight.

1 ounce fresh yeast
⅔ cup milk, warmed
1½ cups bread flour
pinch of salt
¼ cup superfine sugar
3 eggs, beaten
4 tablespoons (½ stick) butter,
softened
⅔ cup golden raisins

FOR THE SYRUP:
1 cup and 2 tablespoons
sugar
1¼ cups water
6 tablespoons rum

1¼ cups cream, freshly
whipped, to serve

Blend the yeast, milk, and a heaping ⅓ cup of the flour in a bowl and leave to stand in a warm place until frothy. Sift the remaining flour and salt into a large bowl and add the sugar. Make a well in the middle and add the frothy yeast mixture and mix with a wooden spoon. Gradually beat in the eggs and butter. Beat the dough well, then cover with a cloth and leave to rise until double in bulk.

Punch down the dough and knead in the golden raisins. Put the dough into four small, greased ring molds, half filling them, and leave to rise again until the dough is level with the top of the mold. Bake in a preheated 400°F oven for 15–20 minutes.

To make the syrup, dissolve the sugar in the water over a low heat for a few minutes. Stir in the rum. When the babas are cooked, leave them to cool in the molds for a few minutes, then turn out and immerse each baba in the hot syrup one at a time. Remove from the syrup and serve immediately with freshly whipped cream.

JP

Tarts of Strawberries

Until the discovery of the new world all we had were the little fraise de bois, or wild strawberries. It took the French to take the red Virginia strawberry, cross it with the large yellow Peruvian, and breed on a different continent what we think of as strawberries. This is a seventeenth-century recipe from Kenelm Digby, but none the worse for surviving the centuries.

FOR THE PASTRY DOUGH:
1½ cups all-purpose flour
pinch of salt
½ cup (1 stick) butter
½ cup lard or vegetable shortening
freshly grated zest of 1 orange

FOR THE FILLING:
½ cup plus 1½ tablespoons superfine sugar
½ teaspoon ground cinnamon
1 teaspoon ground ginger
12 ounces strawberries

To make the pastry dough, sift the flour and salt together. Cut in the butter and lard until the mixture resembles fine bread crumbs. (You can use all butter to make the pastry dough, but the combination of butter and lard makes a crisper crust.) Stir in the orange zest and only a little water. This is very short, so chill it well before rolling out. Use a cookie cutter to cut out linings and lids for individual tart pans.

Mix together the sugar, cinnamon, and ginger. Put your strawberries into the tartlets and sprinkle with this mixture. Cover with a pastry dough lid, and sprinkle on a little more sugar mixture. Bake in a preheated oven at 375°F for 15 minutes.

CDW

Fragomammella (Strawberry Breasts)

(formula by the Futurist Poet of National Record Farfa)
A pink plate with two erect feminine breasts made of ricotta dyed pink with Campari with nipples of candied strawberry. More fresh strawberries under the covering of ricotta, making it possible to bite into an ideal multiplication of imaginary breasts.

From *Futurist Cookbook* by Filippo Tommaso Marinetti
Published by Trefoil Publications Ltd, 7 Royal Parade, London SW6
© Estate of F.T. Marinetti, 1989
English translation ©Suzanne Brill, 1989

Serves 8

1 pound fresh strawberries
1 tablespoon lemon juice
1 tablespoon superfine sugar
1¼ pounds ricotta cheese
⅔ cup heavy cream
3 tablespoons Campari
4–5 tablespoons confectioners' sugar

Set aside sixteen of the smallest strawberries, and cut the rest into small pieces. Put in a bowl with the lemon juice and superfine sugar and leave to soak for 1 hour. Push the ricotta through the smallest strainer of a food mill or a fine sieve. Add the cream and Campari, and mix well. Sift the confectioners' sugar into the mixture to your own taste. Set aside one-third of the mixture and mix the chopped strawberries into the remaining ricotta cheese.

Prepare pink dessert plates, and divide the mixture into sixteen breast-shaped molds, two for each plate, and chill. Unmold the ricotta "breasts" and, using a moistened palette knife, smooth over the reserved ricotta to cover the entire surface. To finish, place a strawberry on the top of each "breast." You can make the molds 3 hours in advance and store in a refrigerator.

JP

Raspberry Shortcake

This is not shortcake in the Scottish sense, but more the American variety which is really like a sponge cake that soaks up all the juices from the berries. Good and gooey, a delight to all children and grownups alike.

1⅓ cups self-rising flour
¼ cup ground blanched almonds
¼ teaspoon salt
½ teaspoon ground cinnamon
6 tablespoons (¾ stick) butter, softened
6 tablespoons superfine sugar
1 egg, beaten
⅔ cup milk
1 tablespoon raspberry jam
⅔ cup heavy cream, lightly whipped
12 ounces fresh raspberries or frozen raspberries, slowly thawed
¼ cup confectioners' sugar

Sift the flour, almonds, salt, and cinnamon into a bowl. Cut in the butter and stir in the sugar. Add the beaten egg and milk to make a biscuit-like dough. Divide dough into halves and gently shape each half to fit into greased 8-inch cake pans.

Bake in a preheated 450°F oven for 10–15 minutes. Remove from the oven and cool on a wire rack.

When cold, spread one of the layers with raspberry jam, then generously with the cream and raspberries. Sprinkle raspberries with half of the confectioners' sugar, cover with the second layer, and top with more cream. Decorate with a few raspberries and sprinkle with the remaining confectioners' sugar. Best eaten when fresh.

JP

Illustrated overleaf

Walnut and Marmalade Teabread

Marian MacNeill surmised that if every French woman was born with a saucepan in her hand every Scots woman was born with a rolling pin. I remember my Aberdonian grandmother saying she was referring to the Scottish ability to bake, not to deal with husbands when they came home drunk! Certainly when I was young it was the great test of a woman's suitability as a daughter-in-law. There is nothing nicer than the smell of baking through the house, and it is one of my objections to microwaves that our children will grow up without the smell of food cooking. This is a very satisfying teabread for a lazy afternoon.

1⅔ cups all-purpose flour
pinch of salt
1 tablespoon baking powder
½ cup (1 stick) butter
¼ cup superfine sugar
½ cup chopped walnuts
finely grated zest of 1 orange
2 eggs, beaten
3 tablespoons marmalade
2–3 tablespoons milk

Grease and carefully line an 8 x 4-inch bread pan. Sift the flour, salt, and baking powder into a bowl. Cut in the butter until the mixture resembles bread crumbs. Stir in the sugar, nuts, and zest. Add the eggs, marmalade and sufficient milk to make a fairly soft batter. Spoon into the bread pan and bake in a preheated 350°F oven for 1¼–1½ hours, or until well risen and golden brown. Turn out and cool on a wire rack.

CDW

Index

12/04--1--12/13/06